Pope John XXIII, 1963, bronze
Collection of Archbishop Capovilla

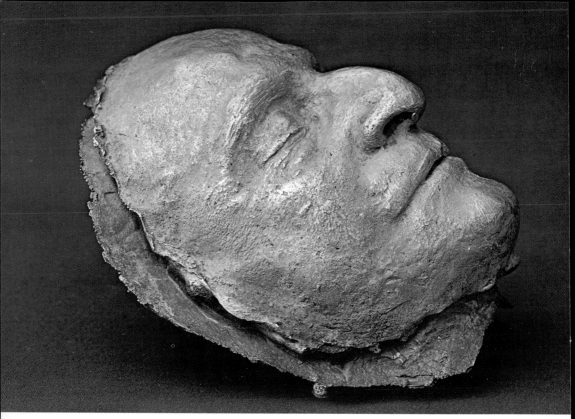

Death mask of Pope John XXIII, 1963, bronze
Collection of Archbishop Capovilla

Hand of Pope John XXIII, 1963, bronze
Collection of Archbishop Capovilla

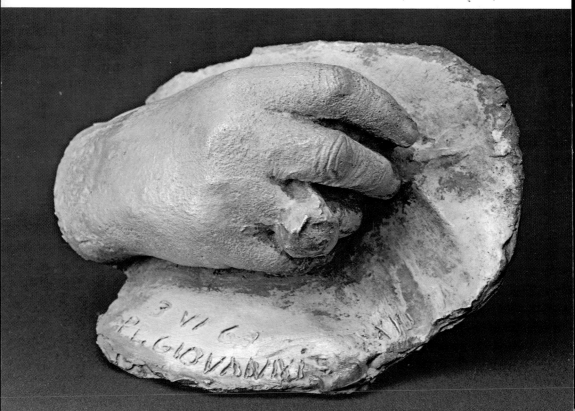

Death of Pope John XXIII
Panel from the Doors of St. Peter's

Pope John XXIII, 1960, guache
Collection of Archbishop Capovilla

An Artist and The Pope

by

Curtis Bill Pepper

based upon the personal recollections of

Giacomo Manzù

Illustrations by Manzù

A GINIGER BOOK
published in association with

MADISON SQUARE PRESS
GROSSET & DUNLAP, INC.
New York

Translations of "Mediterraneo" and "I Limone" are included with the permission of the publishers of *Ossi di Seppio* by Eugenio Montale, copyright 1948 by Arnoldo Mondadori Editore, and New Directions Publishing Corporation, publishers of *Eugenio Montale: Selected Poems*.

Quotation for *The Phenomenon of Man* by Teilhard de Chardin is included by permission of the Estate of Teiihard de Chardin; Harper & Row, Publishers, and Wm. Collins Sons & Co., Ltd., 1959.

Published simultaneously in Canada.

Library of Congress Catalog Card Number: 68-29308

Published by Grosset & Dunlap, Inc.
in association with
The K. S. Giniger Company, Inc.

Printed in the United States of America.

Note to the Reader

This book was written on the basis of Giacomo Manzù's personal recollections, as well as on the basis of other research and original documents.

Acknowledgement should be made by the author to Giacomo Manzù for his help in compiling the material for this book. Long hours before a tape recorder and endless search through scattered notes and old letters robbed the sculptor of his most precious possession — untouched time. Special acknowledgement is also made to Monsignor Loris Capovilla, now Archbishop of Chieti, for invaluable reference to source material.

Giacomo Manzù wishes to add, on his part, his acknowledgement to "the memory of Pope John, the friendship of the late don Giuseppe de Luca and the loving assistance of Inge."

Finally, deep gratitude is extended to Bill and Marcie Free who shared their hearthside, Father Francis X. Murphy who lent his scholarship, and to Beverly Pepper who gave, as always, her heart and her hands.

Curtis Bill Pepper

Contents
and
Illustrations

Color Section   preceding title page

Chapter 1   3
    Cardinale, back and front, 1960

Chapter 2   15
    Inge, 1961

Chapter 3   23
    Study for angels in *Death of the Virgin,* 1961

Chapter 4   33
    Pope John, Manzù, don Giuseppe and Monsignor
    Capovilla, 1961

Chapter 5   49
    Pope John XXIII, 1961

Chapter 6   65
    Pope John and Monsignor Capovilla, 1961

Chapter 7   85
    Don Giuseppe de Luca and Pope John, 1960

Chapter 8   95
    Pope John XXIII, 1963

Chapter 9   103
    Detail study for *Christ in our Humanity*
    and *Pope John,* 1960

Chapter 10   113
    Study for *Christ in our Humanity,* 1950-1960

Chapter 11   129
    Study for *Christ in our Humanity,* 1950-1960

Contents

Chapter 12   143
    Inge and bust of *Pope John*, 1963
Chapter 13   157
    War, 1954
Chapter 14   177
    Study for *Death of Pope John*, 1963
Chapter 15   191
    Pope John and Monsignor Capovilla, 1963
Chapter 16   207
    Portrait study of *Pope John*, 1960
Chapter 17   219
    Death of John XXIII, 1963
Chapter 18   237
    Pope John XXIII, 1961
Photographic Section   following page 122

All photographs are by Mario Carrieri except where otherwise credited.

An Artist
and The Pope

Chapter One

LEAVING the car to climb the steps of St. Peter's, they found a canvas screen had been hung around the grilling of the portico to prevent the public from seeing anything. They had been told there were to be no women, not even their own, and now it was clear there was to be hardly anybody at all: only the Pope with a few courtiers, a couple of German diplomats—and themselves.

They were five from Bergamo, with the sculptor in the middle, and as they climbed the steps he clenched his fists in anger.

"*Porca miseria,*" he said. "What a disgrace."

He had a short figure with the shoulders and neck of a bull, all very compact and hard as though cut from a block of granite—the sound of this breaking rock providing even his name: Manzù. His hands were square, their thick palms swollen from pounding uncounted tons of clay into human form. His face was square, too, with the mouth a wide flat line, clamped shut in anger.

The eyes were something else, separate and apart. No rage seeped into their brown pools, streaked with flecks of green. In the rockhard face, they lay open and exposed without defense, looking at the world with the frank, linger-

3

ing intimacy of a child seeing it for the first time.

"Who would have imagined that this could have happened?" he asked.

"It could be worse," said Mario Zappettini, his brother-in-law. "They could have not put up the doors. They could have hid them in the cellar and washed their hands of the whole thing."

"They wouldn't have dared such a thing," he replied. "Even if some priests in the Curia wanted to try it, they would never have hid my doors because Pope John wanted them and everybody knows it."

"If only Pope John was here," said Mario. "It would be different."

Manzù said nothing and climbed on. Pope John had told him: "Let me know when your doors are finished and we will have a *festa*. We will invite everybody to come to St. Peter's to look at them."

But now John was dead and they had a new Pope and the great bronze doors, where Manzù had left sixteen years of his life, were about to be unveiled—behind a canvas screen, as though they were a source of sudden shame, something unwanted by God or man.

"Giacomo," said Mario. "You have enemies as does every great artist. Michelangelo had to fight like a tiger to build this huge temple to St. Peter. He fought fellow artists and he fought priests. He even fought Popes. He dumped a can of paint on top of one of them."

"All right, all right," he said, hoping his brother-in-law would shut up.

It was a bad example, almost blasphemy. Michelangelo had made history and to talk about him was the same as speaking of Dante or Shakespeare or Einstein— or, in modern art, Matisse and Braque and Picasso. Like Michelangelo, they began immediately, Matisse to be

4

Matisse, Braque to be Braque, Picasso to be himself—that is, to be masters.

So Manzù thought, climbing the steps:

—As for myself, *caro* Mario, the truth is that I will be only one of many who have worked on St. Peter's, one among hundreds who came before me and are now forgotten. But it is just this which allows me to go on working. If I entered my studio in the morning, saying I was a master and about to create something great, I'd be in immediate trouble and do nothing. It's my belief that I am like all other men, and this gives me the faith and strength to keep going.

—Mario was right, however, about my enemies. I had them, all over the place, especially among the cardinals and monsignori in the Pope's governing Curia. For them I was a Marxist and an atheist who voted communist. I was therefore an enemy of religion and morally unfit to do the great doors of St. Peter's. I might have been a friend of Pope John, but he had opened his arms too wide for too many people, including such flaming Reds as the daughter and son-in-law of Nikita Khrushchev. Together with such types, Giacomo Manzù, the atheist artist, had crept into Pope John's Christian embrace for his own unChristian ends.

—So they had said, in seeking to defame me and prevent the doors from being made to bear the life they bear today. While John was alive, however, my enemies had been held back. Yet now we had a different Pope and we were being received in a different way—behind a canvas. He had been given the whispered word and a curtain had gone up.

So thought Manzù, as he climbed the steps of St. Peter's with his friends. At the top, a small group of people stood before the central gate, trying to see inside: Romans, curious about their own backyard, and some pilgrims.

It was the hour of sunset and the basilica was closed. Papal gendarmes opened the gate for the men from Bergamo, then slammed it shut against the others.

Manzù looked back into their faces and saw a young man blinking in wonder, a little girl sitting on her father's shoulders, and a woman asking the guards why she could not also come in. This made him feel even more melancholy. These were the people who had made his doors possible. They were on them. With their flesh and blood, they formed the stuff of the panels. It was all there: their beliefs and doubts, their loves and pain, their dignity — and their dying. Without them, the doors would have no substance — no more than the Church itself. For the Church belonged to the people, not only to the priests and the monsignori. And his doors belonged to the people, not to one Pope or a whispering clutter of courtiers.

"The Holy Father will be here soon," said a monsignor in a purple cape.

Inside the closed area were a dozen clerics and laymen. Most of the priests wore black cassocks and, gathered before the golden doors, they looked about with the vacant stare of people waiting to catch a train. Suddenly the purple-caped monsignor grabbed Manzù's arm and whispered excitedly: "He's left the elevator and gone to St. Peter."

They talked that way in the Vatican. Saints and dead Popes were discussed as though they were next door neighbors, or cousins in another town. And more than anyone else, St. Peter himself was treated as an actual reality. He dwelt within the Church. He was its first rock, and the basilica was built around him — around his tomb, where archaeologists had found the brittle bones of a man without a head. And it was to this sacred spot that Pope Paul had gone to pray, after taking an elevator from his apartment in the Apostolic Palace, then walking across the floor of the basilica to a grilled stairwell leading down to St. Peter's tomb. Every year at this hour, in the month of June, and on the eve of the feast day of St. Peter, the Pope descended the same stairs to pray at the tomb of the saint.

"He's praying above St. Peter now," said the monsignor.

Manzù looked out, over the top of the canvas screen, toward the evening sky. Swallows swung to and fro, stitching twilight onto the night. Let the Pope look into the headless tomb. He, Giacomo Manzù, would look to the sky at sunset—or at the break of day when the slanted hour made it easier to peer through heaven toward infinity. When you studied it, especially at that hour, the order of the sky and the earth was overwhelming. So was everything in it, including light and sound. The roll of waves in an empty seashell, the unfolding heart of a rose, the glistening blue-green wings of a June bug—where did it all come from? What giant matrix turned it all out?

There had to be something behind it all and, little by little, scientific man would be able to see it and eventually hold it in his hands. For man went plunging into the universe, prying open its secrets. He walked and he ran with time by his side, helping him along the way. Time allowed him to make corrections and to take hold. So they went together, man and time, going always toward perfection. Maybe they would reach it in a thousand or a million years—who could say?

Perhaps, too, they would never get there. Perhaps time would outrun man. For he was already slipping. He was losing the sense of the seasons, the taste for silence and the touch of solitude. And without it, he was beginning to flounder, as one falling through space.

The sculptor turned to look at his Death in Space, a lower panel on the doors. Tumbling over and over was a man without a parachute, or perhaps an astronaut unlinked from his spaceship. Yet it was also man without his feet on the ground, man who had lost control of his world and himself, and so went floundering and flailing through time and space—a common figure of our time, falling, falling falling. . .

"Giacomo!" whispered Mario. "Here he comes!"

Pope Paul VI walked toward them, followed by two cardinals and a tiny swarm of monsignori. On his face there was an air of surprise, as though he had just learned of an unusual event about to happen under the portico of his church. It was the look of someone taking the middle road, for there would be no festive, open-air dedication of the doors as Pope John had planned. It would be done at nightfall, behind a canvas wall, with no women and only a few men. Yet this Pope, keeping the outward form of a covenant with his dead predecessor, would be there—with a look of surprise on his face. It was the prudent, Pauline way.

He wore a flaming red cape, a white skullcap and white soutane. He carried his hands chest-high and folded together over a golden pectoral cross—until they were forced open by those rushing to kneel and kiss his fisherman's ring. Some men went down while looking upwards at the Pope's face, as though sinking beneath waves. Others knelt with their eyes fixed only on the ring—amber portal to eternal salvation.

Manzù shook hands, and introduced his son Pio, then his brother-in-law Mario and the banker Raffaele Mattioli, whom the Pope already knew. After that, they walked over to the doors and Pope Paul began to study the panel showing Mary touched by the angels. Then he looked at the body of Jesus being lowered earthward, passing next to the lower panels where he paused finally before the image of Pope John in prayer.

Mattioli leaned close to the Pope and said: "He appears to be a saint in prayer . . . already a saint."

Paul glanced quickly toward the banker, as though this was most startling news, then looked back at Pope John praying. After a moment, he turned to Manzù with a gentle smile and sad eyes. It was a naked, silent moment and in it Manzù felt that if he ever met Paul on the street in civilian clothes, he could only say: "Here is an extremely shy and sensitive man who is incurably sad."

The silence stretched on. Paul waited for Manzù to speak, but the sculptor said nothing. He never spoke in front of his work. So the Pope spoke first.

"If you'd like to explain to us the significance of all those . . . ," said Paul, waving his hand toward the two big panels and the eight smaller ones.

"*Santità*," said Manzù, "I don't think I know the words for this, but I will try."

He began then to explain that the central theme of the doors was Death. Paul knew this anyway, and nodded as if to say so. There was, of course, much more to it than that. For essentially the doors described the living as they took leave of life. It was a bronze world unto itself, filled with saints and sinners, mystics and murderers, Popes and plain people—a cross-section of the endless, swarming, shuffling parade of humanity as it has gone through the one door common to all mankind since the first fratricide. Some crowded through the portal with wonder, others went tumbling and screaming, while still others made the passage with a nod and a prayer. Yet each one in his going attested to the value and dignity and beauty of life. In this sense, the work should have been called the Doors of Life, not Death.

Had Manzù been able, he would have explained this —and much more—to Pope Paul. But he did not feel up to saying such things to him. He could have done it for Pope John, but this was a different Pope. Besides, his chamberlains stood there smirking and frowning, as though the sculptor was about to stumble with his catechism. He plunged onward:

"Above, you see the death of Mary and the death of Christ—those two large panels on top. Then, in the middle, the cut stalks of grapevine and wheat are the symbol of the Eucharist. They are also symbols of life, since there can be neither nourishment, nor rebirth, without death."

He looked at the Pope who blinked once in return, as though staring from a moving train window. Nothing seemed to register.

"Below, are eight little panels showing the death of Abel, the death of Joseph, of Stephen . . ."

Joseph? Stephen? With a shock, Manzù realized he had failed to call them saints. *Porca miseria*. The smirking monsignori had been right to expect a stumble. So he began all over again:

"This is the death of Saint Joseph, this of Saint Stephen and this of Saint Gregory in exile . . . then in these bottom panels is shown death among the faithful . . . there is first death by violence . . ."

He waited for the Pope to ask a question perhaps about that, but there was merely one more blink and a nod.

"In the next panel, there should have been Death in Water. But when I was doing this, Pope John died. So I put him here instead, praying. Then there's Death in Space, and Death on Earth. And here, underneath, are wild creatures of the night and the earth. They don't all represent Christian themes, but I picked them anyway because they give a sense of life and death."

Each one was identified: the dove, the hedgehog, the dormouse, the owl, the crow, and a snake bitten by a tortoise.

Manzù watched the Pope look again at Death on Earth and wondered if he recognized the figure of the woman with her screaming child. Probably he did. Her face was in museums and private art collections around the world. And most certainly, he knew much more than just that.

Finally he spoke: "Weren't there supposed to be some words on each panel to explain them?"

"Yes," replied the sculptor. "Cardinal Testa insisted on this, but I knew from the beginning that it would have done more harm than good. The work seemed clear enough to me without words."

This did not appear to convince Pope Paul. He looked back at the panels as though he would be happier to see Latin phrases under each one. Or on top of them, cluttering the background voids which had been created with great effort to balance the total work.

This embarrassing stall was fortunately broken by two *Sanpietrini* workmen opening the doors. The group walked through in silence, then turned to look at the reverse side, with its lateral strip showing Vatican Council II.

"This is the Council and Pope John receiving Cardinal Rugambwa. Pope John told me Rugambwa was a man of great religious concepts, so I show him kissing John's hand. The others are all cardinals and bishops . . ."

The Pope had spotted, at the extreme left, the figure of a monsignor and, looking at the monsignor with love and concern, was that same woman—the one whom they had not allowed to come with the sculptor for the unveiling of the doors.

"It's Monsignor de Luca . . ."

Pope Paul nodded: he had known him quite well.

11

Manzù then indicated an inscription on the lower right side of the doors—his dedication to a plain priest, and man of culture, on the first doors in 500 years to be hung before the largest church in Christendom:

.TO DON GIUSEPPE
DE LUCA THIS
DOOR OF DEATH IS
DEDICATED — GIACOMO
MANZÙ   1963

"When don Giuseppe de Luca died, I asked Pope John's permission to dedicate the doors to him and he said yes . . ."

"We are content you did this for him," replied Pope Paul.

He began then to talk to the German ambassador to the Holy See and to his friend, the banker Mattioli. Finally, as he was leaving, the Pope turned and said to the waiting sculptor: "God bless you."

He left with his aides, walking through the dark basilica toward the elevator. The other bishops and monsignori soon disappeared, and that was all. No one said another word to the sculptor from Bergamo—not even his friend Monsignor Capovilla for whom he had a special respect and affection. The indifference and hostility were humiliating.

He looked back at the doors and with sadness felt a gulf growing between himself and his work. While making them, they had been an inner part of his being. Now they were on their own. They took with them something of him which he would never have again: years of labor and love, gone from his life, left somewhere in the bronze. They took with them, too, something of the lives of the three people who had made them possible: Pope John who gave his understanding, don Giuseppe his faith, and

Inge her heart. Without them, the great labor would never have been completed.

Above all else, he was proud to have been near a man of immense spiritual balance, who never pretended to have in his hands the monopoly of good or bad, but only of love toward other men—a born priest and true man of God who for some incredible reason was elected Pope and took the name of John.

Chapter Two

Without any knowledge of what was about to happen to him, Giacomo Manzù came to Rome in the spring of 1960 to do a bust of Pope John XXIII. He made the transfer from Milan with haste, expecting to be called to the Vatican almost immediately. The days went by, however, without this happening. So he worked in a studio on the Aventine, doing some figures of seated cardinals and a couple of dancing nudes with free-falling pony tails.

He also had to finish work on a pair of bronze doors forming one portal of St. Peter's, but this went badly. Two variations of one panel, depicting the death of Gregory VII, were not too bad. But everything else connected with the great doors died in his hands, causing him to push it aside in favor of subjects closer to his heart. In this way the days passed, each one pressing gently upon the other like the soft roots of spring—until, one morning in early May, it came to an end.

Manzù awakened that morning to the sound of snipping scissors, below the bedroom window which opened onto the garden. Looking out, he saw a maid picking iris. She had good legs and he could see them best when she hunched

15

down to judge a flower before cutting its ripe, pulpy stem.

The irises were still wet from the night and after collecting them into her apron, their dampness penetrated onto her pink dress. This caused her to hold the apron higher, and so provided a better vision of the dress clinging damply to her splendid body.

A woman, he thought, can be most beautiful where she folds at her belly and thighs. This one, wet with the night and the juice of flower stems, was a magnificent creature. She was between thirty and forty, the age of Venus de Milo, and therefore old enough for every mysterious element and cavern of her body to be linked into one unified instrument for sex and love and birth—and trust. A woman like that was biologically projectable into time beyond one single act of love: a short-lived goddess, glistening with brief immortality. The shape and purpose of her body defeated death today by simply promising more tomorrow.

It was woman at her most exciting age, and Francesco da Barberini had a good eye when he found that her "knees and legs, with both feet on the ground, have in themselves a form that laughs."

She saw Manzù looking at her and knew what was being admired. While it was still in full view, she called up with delightful self-assurance.

"Buon giorno, professore!"

"Buon giorno," he replied, and thought: *"Santo diavolo,* what a splendid way to begin the day!"

Taking a pad, he began to sketch the woman with flowers. He tried several positions, with varying folds of body and apron, then did a satyr looking at her, and another satyr in the act of drawing her. As he began another one of the simple beast making love, Angelo Poliziano's

16

couplet rose up from memory like an encircling garland
of prideful roses:

> *I found myself, young girls, while it was May,*
> *In a green garden, at the break of day.*

Breakfast was laid out, but he was too excited to take
more than a gulp of black coffee before hastily beginning
a pencil drawing of Inge.

She sat before the window. How many times had he
drawn and sculpted that face, yet never exhausted its won-
ders? There was this morning a fragment of sleep in her blue
eyes and her lips seemed swollen from the taste of love.
Sketching her, he covered her robe with a shower of flowers.

"They look like daisies," she said.

The features of a woman, he thought, were little
echoes of her body. You can't separate them . . .

"I like violets," she said.

. . . and all the echoes and chambers were to be taken
together, for they were all of woman.

"You don't remember they were violets."

"Where?"

"At my feet. That day."

She was talking about their first meeting, but she
had mistaken the flower. It had happened in Salzburg,
at the Summer Academy, where the ballerinas from the
opera house came to pose for Manzù's sculpture class
and also on the floor above for Oscar Kokoschka, who
gave lessons in water-color and painting. One afternoon
there was no model for Manzù and he said to his assistant:

"*Santo cielo!* What'll we do now?"

"Never mind, Kokoschka has lent us his."

"*Va bene,*" he said. "Fine."

17

The model came and as soon as Manzù saw Inge, he knew she was ideal. Though dressed—none of the dancers posed in the nude—it was clear that she possessed a rare body and a most unusual face. She had to stay.

"Listen," he said to his assistant. "Don't allow that *signorina* to go away from us until the school term has ended. Send our model up to Kokoschka and we will keep his."

It was the first time something like that had happened to him. He had taught for fourteen years, since 1940, without ever becoming involved with a model. But with Inge, from the first day, it was different. Her face and form rushed upon him, the sculptor, filling voids and creating others. She caught his eyes and seemed to accept all they meant with joy, as though she had been created for this alone and only through it could she ever live. That was how they felt, almost immediately, without saying anything.

Finally, one morning he came to class to find her posing, on her toes, in a ballet dress. The classroom was large and filled with students, but he walked over to her as though they were alone in the room—and left a flower at her feet.

That was how it had begun in Salzburg. But it was, he recalled, a single rose and not a bunch of violets.

"Giacomo, don't you remember?"

"Yes, of course, Inge."

Afterwards, she came to Milan to pose for him. Their friendship grew ever closer, until it became what it is today—his companion in work and the love of his life.

The phone rang and rang again. The maid did not answer it and Inge jumped up. As she went through the door, something told Manzù that he was about to be brutally yanked from his green garden in the middle of May.

18

"It's Monsignor de Luca," she said, returning.

He watched her, and suddenly realized he wanted to try doing a series on models undressing. It had been turning about inside him for some time, yet only now was it clear that he wanted it. Inge caught him watching her and knew what it was and smiled at the thought of it.

"Giacomo, he's waiting . . ."

Going to the phone, he had another feeling that the rhythm of his days was about to be broken—and he was right.

"Pope John wants to see you tomorrow."

"See me?"

"He will sit for you tomorrow at three-thirty, so you can do your bust of him."

De Luca sounded very pleased, but Manzù did not.

"What's wrong, Giacomo?"

"Nothing, nothing, don Giuseppe."

"Are you still having trouble with the doors?"

"No trouble at all—I've simply stopped work on them."

"Why?"

"Because I can't do them."

"I think," said de Luca, "that I should come over. I'm very nearby."

"There's not much to say," he replied.

"We should discuss your meeting with the Pope, anyway."

"All right—come over now if you want."

He hung up and walked to his studio. It wasn't far: a few steps around the corner and through a gate into the Torlonia gardens where a high vaulted arch of a Roman temple had been covered to preserve it from the weather. The result of this noble effort was an unusual enclosure— not large in area, but over 32 feet high, with deep windows on each side. It made an ideal workshop for the doors whose height of 25 feet required an exceptionally high working area.

But Manzù did not want to talk to Monsignor de Luca about the doors. They hinged on a faith which he no longer possessed. There was no use discussing it because it was gone from him and no words could bring it back, not even those of don Giuseppe who was more than brother and closer than father.

Manzù did not look upon de Luca as a priest. He was more than that—a man whose learning and compassion and grace he admired above all other men. He believed in him as a human being and de Luca, in turn, believed in the sculptor and respected him.

There was one major difference: de Luca had a faith which Manzù no longer possessed. The sculptor, at 49, had created in his brief years an army of cardinals and a score of Christs. They were scattered around the world, in museums, homes and churches. He had done the bronze doors for the Salzburg Cathedral and, when commissioned to do the doors of St. Peter's, he began them believing they would be a great labor of his life. Yet that was 12 years ago, and before finishing them, his faith had gone. It had been crumbling, like a castle, for years and now there was nothing but a heap of stones on a hill beneath a low sky. He was no longer a Catholic. He did not believe in the Church, and God's existence was a matter which did not concern him.

Suddenly, as one walking in a dream, Manzù found himself in the flower garden. He had walked past his studio, without entering, and continued into the interior garden where that morning he had seen the woman picking flowers.

She was gone, without a trace of where she had knelt

to cut the wet stems and receive the sweet liquids of night. He saw then a footprint in the flower bed and bent to study its form, thinking how much life there was in the simple impression of one woman's foot . . .

"*Buon giorno, professore!*"

Startled, he looked up into the wrinkled face of an old gardener.

"*Buon giorno,*" he replied, and then heard the jingling of the front door bell. It was don Giuseppe, arriving to discuss the date with Pope John and, against his wishes, that great, stalking ghost of his life—the unfinished doors for St. Peter's.

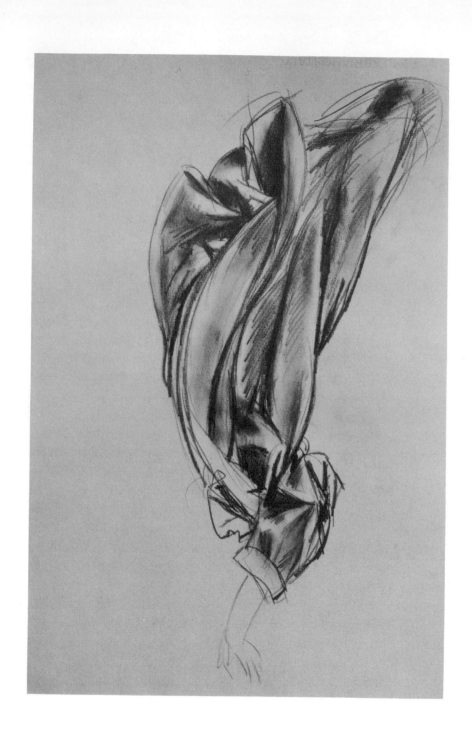

Chapter Three

Don Giuseppe was inside the gate, peering up at a bay tree through his thick eye-glasses.

"I just saw a bluebird," he said.

"Certainly—spring has come."

"This is paradise," he said, with a sigh.

"It's a green garden, at the break of May. And Eve was here this morning."

"Eve?"

"Ready to nibble once more on the forbidden fruit."

Don Giuseppe smiled happily. Eternal Eve obviously interested him more than passing bluebirds. Both men stood before the studio door in leaf-splattered sunlight, the priest a head taller than the Bergamasque. Around them was bird song and, beyond the wall, somewhere in the street, a woman laughed — followed by a car motor starting.

"She was beautiful. You should have seen her . . . the body of a Venus."

"How shameful!" cried don Giuseppe, full of delight.

"And I was just as greedy as Adam to taste the fruit."

"Adam wasn't greedy," replied don Giuseppe, suddenly concerned. "It was Eve. The serpent said the fruit would make her a goddess and she ate it because she was jealous and ambitious. Poor Adam expected her to die. They'd

23

been told touching the tree meant death and so he saw
two possibilities: life without Eve or risking death doing
what she did. He loved her too much to lose her, so he
took his chance and ate the fruit."

"A great and noble gesture," said Manzù, "for which
he was kicked out of paradise. You priests rant about
love, yet how much does it really mean to you?"

"It means everything, but Adam went too far. He
loved Eve more than God. He gave her an infinite love, which
is reserved for God alone. And so he overstepped his mark.
Adam admits this to Dante when they meet in paradise: 'the
tasting of the tree was not by itself the cause of so great
an exile, but only the overpassing of the bound.' "

Manzù shook his head.

"You're wrong," he said. "Love doesn't come in little
parcels. It stretches out without fences. When it's real, it's
infinite. Otherwise it isn't love."

"No, it's a matter of order. Adam loved Eve in a dis-
orderly way."

"Listen, don Giuseppe, how do you think people
love? Woman isn't subordinate to any prefixed system
of God or anyone else. Our natural state is pure, limpid
and blameless. It needs no document or blessing—civil
or religious."

"I'm saying it's not how or what people do, Giacomo.
It's what they *don't* do . . . what they leave out. Adam
loved Eve to the exclusion of God."

"Which is the only way a man can really love—totally,
excluding all else. And Eve . . . did she love Adam that
much?"

"It seems obvious," said don Giuseppe, "that she was
rather bored in the garden."

"Also typical," said Manzù, both men laughing easily
as he opened the studio door.

"There they are!" exclaimed don Giuseppe, looking upward.

The sculptor looked down and took a deep breath. Immediately before them was a field of figures in work—dancers, cardinals, two busts of Inge with a headscarf, and a low relief of a nude seated in the lap of a bearded painter.

Don Giuseppe paid these little heed, however, threading his way with surprising grace past a pony-tailed dancer and a small cardinal, coming finally to the full-scale, snow-white plaster models of St. Peter's doors.

"Che bello!" he murmured, hands clasped with joy.

Before them was the result of 13 years' struggle. It stood 25 feet by 11 and looked twice as big. It was to have been the final model, until Manzù decided against it, despite don Giuseppe who liked the work and had helped it come into being over the years, counseling at every turn and with each successive model.

More than this, the priest had been Manzù's protector, defending him from monsignori and cardinals in the Roman Curia who were against the sculptor doing the doors of St. Peter's. Manzù had been condemned by the Holy Office. He did naked Christs and naked Madonnas. He was a Communist—worse, he was Satan with a sculptor's chisel. So they said, without knowing the whole truth.

Don Giuseppe had buttonholed these faceless inquisitors and explained otherwise. He had even published an art edition of Manzù's final study for the doors—an extremely daring act for anyone in the Curia, since a pulled button can be sewn back on, but a printed word can never be erased. Finally, his faith and support ignited a campaign in the Italian press, testifying that Giacomo Manzù was the sculptor best equipped to create the great basilica doors.

That won the battle. The Pontifical Commission

for Sacred Art was constrained to accept the sculptor from Bergamo. And in exchange, he accepted the theme of the doors: The Glorification of the Saints and Martyrs of the Church. Yet many things had happened since then, and now he was unable to continue the work.

It sat there, like an unwanted member of a household whose presence could neither be enjoyed nor removed. The only defense against such an obstacle is to cease looking at the whole person, concentrating instead on one or another object: a nose, a cane, a wart, a bosom, an old ring, a turned back — creating small battlefields where it is easy to marshal sufficient forces of hate or love to secure a desired emotion and so achieve co-existence with a minimum of effort.

So it was with the doors of Manzù. He saw what he liked. Some of the lower panels were not too bad, such as the death of St. Gregory or St. Joseph. He could understand the death of a Pope in exile or an old man dying by the road. The stoning to death of St. Stephen interested him, too, because of its violence.

But he could not look at the upper panels, intended as the crowning glory of the doors. In one, Mary was assumed bodily into heaven as Eve looked up in ecstasy. And in the companion panel, Christ sat triumphant in the sky, above a wonderous, earthbound throng which included Adam.

"Christ and Mary in Paradise," said don Giuseppe. "You have resolved it beautifully."

He had not — not according to his way of looking at it, because he was neither God, nor a prophet. He had resolved some difficult problems relating to the spacing of the panels. And by eliminating frames and inscriptions a few voids had been created which echoed surprisingly well the action within them. But resolve Christ and Mary in Paradise—what nonsense!

"No," he said. "It doesn't go."

"What doesn't?"

"Christ and Mary. I can't do that."

"You can't do what?"

"Put them in heaven. I can't just sit them up in the sky like that. I'm sorry, but you know I didn't suggest it. It was not my idea."

"Giacomo, just where do you suppose that Christ and Mary are?"

Having asked that question, don Giuseppe looked up at the top panels, as if to prove that Christ and His mother were indeed up in the sky. Manzù shook his head and turned away, facing toward a nude dancing girl, her feet open duck-style—and flat on the ground.

"I don't know if they are anywhere. The fantasy of man can give birth to Christ and Mary—even Heaven and Hell. But it's a legend for me and I can't say otherwise in my work . . . and you know it."

"Do you believe that Christ existed?"

"Yes, like all other men."

"And that He was exceptional, above the normal man?"

"Yes, all revolutionaries are exceptional men."

"Well, that is what you show here. He exists above other men. What is wrong with that?"

"I listen to you, don Giuseppe, as always, but this explanation doesn't mean anything to me for what I must do. As you know, themes don't create a work of art—only inspiration does and your arguments just don't inspire me."

"Nobody asks you to establish the sense or truth of where they are, but merely to bear witness to the Catholic belief that this is what happened."

"But I don't believe it and I can't. Despite this, you want me to testify for Catholics that these events really happened. That's a priest for you!"

"But what can't you believe?"

"That they went up into heaven, that Christ sits up in the sky, and that Heaven is a piece of Christian real estate."

"Why do you stick to that point?" asked don Giuseppe. "Actually, Jesus lives on this earth. He is in the hearts of people. He came here, He walked our roads, He lived between our walls, and He finally died to continue to live on in the Eucharist and in our hearts. It is a lofty ideal and you have shown it here."

Manzù turned from the dancing girl to face the priest. He had been shoved into a corner and he did not like it.

"There is more than this," he said.

"Perhaps, but nothing loftier, or more sublime."

"Noble and sublime, like your hopes—but they remain that, closed in themselves. Listen, if you were born in Asia, you might have been a Buddhist or a Hindu, right?"

"Yes."

"But you were born in Italy and are a Catholic."

"Yes."

"What makes you think you were born in the right place?"

"I was graced by the accident of birth, to be able to bear witness to the truth."

"And elsewhere, there is nothing to equal it?"

"It is different, and thus not equal."

"That is where we split, don Giuseppe. I cannot exclude the possibility of finding it elsewhere—that truth can be found outside the Catholic faith."

"And inside what?"

"In time and in the going of man into the future."

"No, Giacomo, the epicenter is outside man. By

28

looking inward, man cuts himself off from himself, from other men, and from God. He becomes a man alone, alienated and lost. It is the great ailment of our time."

Manzù wadded some clay in his hand and furiously drove it into another formless mass next to the sculpture, then he turned to face his friend the priest.

"You think we are alienated because we dared to walk out through your church doors, looking for an answer elsewhere? We did this to find answers you could not give us. We are not lost because we are looking. The lost ones are those who stayed behind and half-heartedly accept a God in whom they can no longer believe."

"But you believe. I know you do. An artist's soul such as yours cannot but believe in Christ and God."

"Look, don Giuseppe, stop fooling yourself and leave me as I am. My position has its particular arguments, too. They may not be as powerful as yours, but they exist within me. And they bring their quota of pain, too. Don't think it's easy not to believe. In fact, it would often be easier the other way. I could solve many problems with faith. Instead, I feel compelled to do it through my own conscience, because faith does not exist for me. So please stop nagging me about it!"

Manzù had never before raised his voice to the gentle priest and now it was as though he was shoving him off a cliff. But don Giuseppe only smiled and placed both hands on the sculptor's thick shoulders.

"Do as you like, Giacomo. I only ask that we remain friends as we are at this moment."

Manzù nodded dumbly and they embraced. In doing it, he felt a rush of warmth for this man who had been so kind to him. Was the priest just as lonely as he was? Behind his faith, did he not also have doubts—so that the two of them were but a reverse impression of the

29

same work? Why else did they now cling to one another?

They were, he decided, two protagonists and they acted out their true selves in each other's arena, each one enabling the other to say yes, or no—or simply laugh—and so identify himself. It was a fair exchange. In his appeal for friendship don Giuseppe had admitted it and Manzù liked him even more for it.

They parted and, as happens with men after such a close confession, there were some moments of silence. The priest looked listlessly at the nude dancing girl, then at the grey-green clay form of a seated cardinal, wrapped in moist cellophane. Beyond this was a low relief of a nude seated in the lap of a painter, and he peered at this for a moment.

"Are you ready for the Pope tomorrow?"

"Yes. I'm ready to do my work."

"He won't ask more of you."

Manzù nodded. He had a sudden sensation that he was heading for trouble—deep trouble. But then he shrugged it off. Pope John certainly would not ask what he thought about God. Or Karl Marx. Or modern man, alienated and alone. Or Christ and the Madonna. So what could go wrong? He would set his tripod before him, make the clay bust in one or two sittings—and that would be the end of it. At least, that is what he told himself.

Chapter Four

THE next afternoon don Giuseppe came by in his black Sunbeam to take his friend to Pope John. They loaded up the tripod, some tools and a box of clay, then drove down the Aventine hill to the Tiber. From there, on the far side of the river, could be seen the great dome of St. Peter's. And somewhere within its great shadow, a Pope was preparing to sit for Giacomo Manzù— the son of an impoverished shoemaker who also fed his family by sweeping church floors.

"How long will it take you?"

"I don't know. Two, maybe three, sittings. You know when you start, but never when you will finish."

His father once cleaned the floors of Sant'Alessandro in Bergamo. He arranged the seats in ordered rows and at funerals he carried the cross to the graveside. When he was ill or had to repair shoes, he sent his son Giacomo to clean the church floor and to carry the cross. There were eight children—not counting six who died in infancy— and every lira had its measured weight.

His life was a triangle of home, school and church-cemetery. Other children kidded him, saying he was conceived in the sacristy, between one function and another. Giacomo

33

envied those boys. They played in a happy world of tad-
poles, pigtails and snow slopes—a world he saw only from
one or another corner in the sad, silent triangle of his life.

But he could dream within his triangular world—dreams
as big as thunderhead clouds coming over the old city on
top of the hill where the rich lived in great *palazzi*, dreams
fed by intermittent fears and anxieties. Sometimes he would
awaken at night, trembling with the thought that he would
never be big enough to escape from the valley. He would
go then to fields above the town, to pick wild greens for
the rabbits they kept behind the church. He was happiest
then, walking across the high flatland, close to the scud-
ding clouds. In the spring he also picked violets, pressing
their fragrance against his nose, his eyes, his ears—shyly
hiding them later because it meant a waste of time better
spent gathering rabbit food.

"I told them you wanted the Holy Father to sit on a
raised seat near the window."

"*Grazie.*"

"Because the light has to be always the same—no?"

"*Sì, grazie.*"

After the war, Spanish influenza killed many. As the
bodies piled up, extra hands were needed to put them into
boxes and cart them to the cemetery. He was only nine then,
but they used him to help load the dead and push them to
the open pits. One day a nurse gave him some wine—too
much, and he fell asleep on a return trip from the grave-
yard, curled up inside the coffin wagon.

These dead were the first nudes he could study. Their
gaping mouths, their blue limbs stuck doll-like onto swollen bodies, formed the models of his first anatomy class.
Life had moved out with frightening finality, leaving behind corpses like abandoned homes. He began to draw them,
seeking to return once again to their inert forms some of

life's mysterious substance which had rushed out with the speed of a departing wind.

What power there was in the hand of the artist! And what daring in his heart! Their apartment was next to a convent and when the nuns were inside singing to organ music, he would sneak over to try painting frescoes on their courtyard walls. Once he had done that, the walls ceased being walls and became immense picture frames. *Per bacco!* If he had enough paint, he could paint the walls of the world and so pull them all down.

Such action fed his hopes and these fed a sense of strength and certainty. Nude figures, mainly women and children in pencil and charcoal, began to pour from him—unexpected and unseeded flowers in a home as barren as the Altamira caves.

So it went until one day they chopped it off, taking him from school to begin work. At nine and a half, he was apprenticed to a carpenter. Without further schooling and no desire on his part, he passed from carpenter to woodcarver, from gilder to stucco-worker—until he was 19. So the triangle of his life changed one of its basic elements to become: home—work—church-cemetery . . . home—work—church-cemetery.

"The only person who can approve your work is the Pope himself. It's to be his official portrait. If he likes it, that's all there is to it. So you don't have to worry about any senile old cardinal sticking his nose into your clay pot."

"Yes, so you told me . . . *grazie.*"

The letter asking him to do the work had come from the Papal Secretary of State when he was in bed, in Bergamo, recovering from an illness. It was January. There was snow in the streets and the sound of ice falling from the rooftops.

Inge brought in the letter: would Giacomo Manzù of

Bergamo accept a commission to do a bust of His Holiness, Pope John XXIII?

At first he hesitated—still bitter from attacks launched by cardinals and monsignori in the Roman Curia who had tried to prevent him from doing the doors of St. Peter's. And then, getting the commission to do the doors, he was unable to finish them. So why ask for more? He did portraits only rarely now and mainly of women whose features were interesting. To do a Pope would mean a great deal to a Catholic, but he no longer believed. He had even decided to stop doing cardinals. There was more life and meaning in one dancer's foot than in twenty cardinals whose challenge to him as an artist was now exhausted.

Despite all this, he accepted, writing a letter agreeing to do the work when next in Rome—telling himself this was not an examination of conscience, nor a profession of faith. It was to be a portrait of a human being, one of the most important figures of our time. It was a study of a man, not a bishop. Finally, don Giuseppe had promised that the cardinals would leave him alone on this one.

"You will work up there in the *Biblioteca*—the library where he receives heads of state and holds private audiences."

"The top floor?"

"No, that's his private apartment. No one goes there. It's next to the top. The third floor."

They had reached Piazza San Pietro, with don Giuseppe pointing to the Apostolic Palace. The car moved on, past the great flat face of the basilica, top-heavy with stone saints against the sky, eventually turning into the tunnel of the Arch of the Bell. Swiss Guards saluted them going in and Papal gendarmes waved them onward into Vatican City.

On the left appeared a cemetery with tall black cypresses growing among grey gravestones. This suddenly vanished as the car sped under another arch and then through sunlight around the rear of St. Peter's, where the back of the basilica rose upward, massive and imperious, like the butt-end of a bull-shaped mountain—rooted in rock to the bowels of the earth, and holding within it somewhere the grave of St. Peter.

They drove through other medieval arches, dripping with overhead spikes, then past more orange-red-blue Swiss Guards, turning finally into another long tunnel which ran downward, as though plunging into a dungeon. Finally, the black car emerged into the sunlight of the Belvedere Courtyard, where they parked to take the elevator up to the papal library.

"You'll like Pope John. You are both from Bergamo. For you, it will be like coming home."

"My home, *caro amico*, was never like this."

"I mean, he makes everybody feel that way. As though they all came from the same hometown."

Don Giuseppe had known Pope John before his election to the papacy. When Angelo Roncalli was cardinal-primate of Venice, don Giuseppe had published his study of Cardinal Cesare Baronio. Their friendship, and mutual interest in Church saints and scholars, had continued after Roncalli became John XXIII.

"He never forces a situation, he never pushes you against the wall, and he challenges no one to battle. Yet he wins all the time."

"That happens with Popes."

"But he wins without pulling papal rank. He does it through the power of his own personal example. He has such strength of faith that everything collapses before it."

"Except, I hope, sculptors."

Don Giuseppe smiled, indicating he finally understood it was not the moment to discuss the qualities of Pope John. Shortly, in a few minutes, the sculptor would meet him in a total and enveloping extension of sense and self—first step in doing a portrait. He had to think now about himself and make sure he was clear and strong and able to freely use all his ability to do what was expected of him. To do this, he needed to be silent.

"I told him you were an important artist."

"You shouldn't have done that. I don't consider myself important or even an artist. Picasso is an artist. I am an artisan . . ."

Don Giuseppe smiled again, this time to shut him up.

"Did you also tell him how I see things?"

"He knows only that you are an artist. He probably suspects that you, like millions of other men and women, have become alienated from your faith. That is not unique. Unfortunately it is all too common."

The implication was clear. Pope John knew all about him and his way of thinking. Don Giuseppe had told the Pope in order to protect them from some Curia monsignori and cardinals who would villify them if possible through distortion, slander or any other means.

Two valets helped carry the equipment to the elevator. At the second loggia, a chamberlain led the way to a small office where they met Monsignor Loris Capovilla, the Pope's private secretary. Later, Manzù came to know and admire him. But on this first day, he was too preoccupied with his job to think of anything else.

Capovilla took them down a narrow, low-ceilinged corridor and through a door. Suddenly, without warning, they found themselves in front of Pope John.

"Here we are!" said the Pope.

He stood just inside the door, a short, dumpy figure

38

in white with big ears and a big smile on his face and his arms extended as though ready for an embrace.

"Good day, *Santità*," said Manzù, taking his hand.

Don Giuseppe knelt to kiss the ring, but the Pope quickly pulled him up for a fraternal embrace. Then he turned to the sculptor.

"I see you have an excellent guide," he said. "That's very clever, because this is a complicated place. It's difficult to get into it—and impossible to get out, especially if they make you Pope."

"That's one risk," replied Manzù, "which clearly doesn't threaten me."

They laughed and Pope John said: "You'd never fool me. I'd know you were from Bergamo, even if we spoke Italian."

Only then did Manzù realize they had been speaking the dialect of Bergamo without his being aware of it. Don Giuseppe caught this surprise and they exchanged a smile. It was, as he had said, like coming home again.

Pope John nodded to indicate he was ready—but before beginning, Manzù felt compelled to be frank about the work.

"*Santità*, I've been called to do this portrait, yet I must admit a truth. I've done some portraits, yes. But those two or three which seem good enough for me are of women. I've never done men. I did one of a friend, but only because he was a friend. I did another one, and destroyed it. So the few busts I've done are practically all of women."

The Pope pursed his lips as if to say this was nothing.

"Let's try it," he said. "What difference does it make?" Then with a tug at his white cassock, he added: "After all, if you look at me, you can see I'm also dressed a little bit like a woman."

They all laughed again, the Pope most of all, while Manzù glanced around the immense library to discover that nothing had been prepared for him. Before them was a semi-circle of red and gold armchairs. The central one, resting on a low, portable platform, was obviously a throne seat for the Pope when meeting important visitors.

"That will be fine," he said, "if we can move it next to the window for light."

Pope John talked with don Giuseppe while Capovilla had two ushers move the throne chair. Then the tripod, tools and clay were brought in, made ready, and the Pope took his seat before the sculptor. A servant slid a red velvet cushion under his feet, but he did not seem to enjoy it and kicked it aside. Then, with a resigned sigh, he extended a red-slippered foot and pulled it back. He saw Manzù watching him and both men smiled immediately—their first mutual unspoken confidence.

"May I move about a little bit?"

"Let it be as though I were not here, *Santità.*"

"What do you wish me to wear on my head?"

In his hands he held a *camauro*—the old-fashioned cap, once worn by Popes.

"That will do fine."

"You see, *Monsignore!*" exclaimed Pope John to his secretary. "He says it looks all right on me."

He looked warmly at Manzù, his brown eyes twinkling.

"They don't like this hat too much around here. But you know how it is in these places . . ."

With that, he pulled it on. The red velvet cap, with white ermine trimming, covered part of his high forehead and tops of his large peasant ears. Don Giuseppe stood on the other side of the seated figure, next to a velvet window curtain.

Manzù began to work, only to be interrupted by the Pope: "Is it all right to talk?"

"As though I were not here," he replied, assuming the Pope would talk to don Giuseppe.

"Then I will tell you about how I met your father and what a favor he did for me."

A rough clay form, shaped like an immense light bulb, had been prepared on the armature atop the tripod. As the Pope talked, Manzù worked at this primal shape, adding clay to it.

"It was shortly after my ordination," began Pope John. "As a priest I was still inexperienced and very nervous when talking to groups of people. So when the parish priest of your splendid Sant'Alessandro asked me to give a sermon, I agreed—but with fear I would not do well. I had already had one disaster, with my first lecture, at my Roman seminary, where Father Francesco Pitocchi convinced me to give a little talk to the Children of Mary. I wrote it out beforehand, but upon reading, it seemed too fancy, too flowery and full of high-sounding words. So I made it simpler, and went to give the talk—only to find it was in a rich and fancy place. This confused me and I lost my tongue and, alas, my memory."

The Pope's rambling story also confused Manzù. Unable to follow the Pope, and also concentrate on his work, he stopped to listen. This caused John to wave him back to his tripod.

"No," he said, "go on with your work. Well . . . my talk was a disaster. I mixed up citations from the Old and New Testaments. I confused St. Alfonsus with St. Bernard, I mistook writings of Church doctors for words of the prophets. What a fiasco! I was so ashamed that after it was over I fell into the arms of Father Francesco and confessed my mortification."

A flash bulb went off, startling both Pope and sculptor. A photographer had been admitted to the library and began encircling them with exploding flashes. Manzù looked at him with unconcealed annoyance. The Pope saw this immediately and ceased talking while waiting for the photographer to finish. When he was gone, Pope John continued:

"So, as a young priest, I prepared another speech for the good people of Bergamo . . . but not without concern, fearing that something else would go wrong. It was to be my first sermon in Bergamo, before my family, my relatives and those faithful who had come with trust and love to hear a young servant of our great mother Church. It was at vespers, on the feast day of St. Francis de Sales, in 1906, and with me went the good papa Manzù, who took me to the pulpit . . ."

Besides sweeping the floor and arranging the seats, Manzù's father was also expected to accompany the preacher to the pulpit, wait for him to finish, then take him back to the sacristy.

"I began my sermon, full of doubts about myself, while papa Manzù sat waiting on the pulpit stairs. A sermon in those days ran 40 minutes to one hour and so I kept at it. Halfway through, I grew nervous about how it was going. The faces of the faithful before me were blank and I paused, looking at them with sinking heart. At that moment, I felt a tug at my soutane, but paid it no heed. There was another tug, then another, and finally I turned about to see it was Manzù at my feet, pulling my hem. '*Forza*, don Angelo!' he called 'Keep going, you're doing fine!'"

"That gave me the courage to go ahead and I did much better, thanks to the little bit of help. I've never forgotten it. A small hand to those in doubt can do the work of a giant."

Manzù thanked him for telling the story and pictured his father, sitting on the pulpit stairs at the foot of the young priest, looking up at him. He could see his face and that peculiar little nod he gave when he wanted to show he was with you all the way. When he was not, it was hard for him to look at you at all. And if he was at his cobbler's last, he would often put nails in his mouth which rendered conversation impossible.

One day his mother sent him for money to buy food, and he found his father putting heels on a pair of old work shoes. As soon as he asked for money, the old man put nails in his mouth so that he would not have to say that he had none, shaking his head and refusing to look up. He left him that way, pounding away at the shoe, but once outside, he heard the pounding cease. He wanted to go back then and take the nails out of his father's mouth and say to him that he understood how painful it was for him to not have money for his family. But he did not do it, maybe because no one in their family ever talked that way to one another.

Once he did try to break through the nails. After they had taken him from school and shoved him into a carpenter's shop, he came home one day to tell his father how much he hated it and how he wanted to return to school and study art. But before he could speak, the old man threw a handful of nails into his mouth. Angry and determined to have an answer, he stood there, waiting for his father to use up all the nails. At first he met fierce and menacing stares. But then, as the nails diminished, he saw in his father's eyes a look of unbearable sadness and when asked to do a senseless errand, he left immediately without saying another word. So that was his father—able to tug encouragement at the hem of a priest, but not at the sleeve of his son.

The Pope had gone on talking and Manzù sought to catch his words: ". . . and now the son of the man who helped me preach my sermon, is making my portrait, as well as the great bronze doors for the Church!"

Santo Dio, he thought, how many ghosts were they going to have with them? Both were equally dead—his father and the doors of St. Peter's. If the Pope did not know this, sooner or later he would have to tell him.

John fell silent and Manzù turned back to his work

with the intention of finishing it as quickly as possible. He was worried by what he had seen. The Pope's face had an incredible mobility. From one moment to the next, from one thought to the other, the features shifted radically. This, he realized, was not going to be easy.

Don Giuseppe and the Pope began to discuss a new saint, Gregorio Barbarigo, who was to be proclaimed shortly. Don Giuseppe praised him as a modern priest and described his cultural attainments. Pope John agreed but said there was more involved than just culture, because Barbarigo had "the exquisite and pure spirit of a saint."

Manzù wondered what that was. Then he stopped listening and the work progressed without further disturbance. But as he advanced, his first apprehensions became more real and disturbing. He was heading for trouble. The Pope's face altered from one moment to the next with the rapidity of a child's. It varied according to what he was thinking or talking about. A serious, pensive look would be shattered by a laugh—quickly resettling, but without the same plain alignment. Or his face would alter from certainty to doubt—from looking out, to looking in—changing continually as though seen through a moving prism.

Ordinarily, Manzù could quickly find the inner substance of a subject, or at least that which interested him. If he knew it reasonably well, or had observed it sufficiently, the work could go fast—in an hour and a half, or even less. Also older people, with the deep lines of age, were usually easier. Yet the mobility of this face left him floundering.

It was maddening. Which among the passing faces was the real one? Which was the true Pope, the simple priest, the pastor? Which the inner man?

He had to know this in order to sculpt the head. Yet the only way to obtain it was to see him, the man himself in relation to a variety of subjects—those prime ones which turned his thoughts, his personality, his spirit.

This required spending more time with him, however—and how could he ask for that? A Pope was a prisoner of Vatican ritual, fixed to the rock of protocol like a rock-chained Prometheus. From the day of his election until his death, he was inescapably committed to meet millions of pilgrims, bishops and visitors flooding into Rome. They came without end from around the world, and the Pope had no place to hide from them. He was there to meet them—one and all. So how could a fumbling sculptor expect other than a few sittings?

This realization depressed Manzù. And causing even greater despair, Capovilla gave a sign to call a halt in the day's work—little more than one hour after they had begun.

The sculptor nodded that he understood, and stopped. He had the substance of a portrait, but it was too literal, too benign. It was a happy Pope. The shifting face had left him at the surface. He had not gone deep enough below those large features and the enormous ears. He had not reached the lodestone of loneliness and sacrifice or whatever had to be eventually found.

The Pope, who had sat on the far side of the work and so was unable to see anything, now came around to look at it.

"*Beh*," he said, and nodded his head. "Good . . . good."

Manzù shook his head.

"Not yet, *Santità*."

John looked back at it again, as if to find what was not yet right.

"I know little, if anything, about art," he confessed. A portrait, I suppose, should look like a portrait. But the principal person who must be satisfied is yourself. If you are content, then we will be."

"*Grazie*, that's most kind," replied the sculptor, surprised to find him so gentle and generous. How, he wondered, was such a man ever elected Pope? He even seemed to sense the need to return to the unfinished work as quickly as possible, for he then turned to Monsignor Capovilla.

"We can come again tomorrow, no?"

"*Si, Santità,*" replied his secretary.

There was a moment's silence. Then Pope John put his hand on Manzù's arm.

"If you have no other immediate appointment, why not come with me to see where I live?"

Madonna, had he sensed the need for this, too? Had he seen still further, reading all the fears?

"Perhaps you'd prefer to come some other time?"

"No, *Santità,* it would be a pleasure to come . . . now."

61

Chapter Five

Before leaving with the Pope, Manzù covered his work, wrapping it in a wet towel and cellophane to keep the clay moist. This done, it became necessary to clear it from the room where the Pontiff met his cardinals, bishops and heads of state. Monsignor Capovilla suggested hiding it behind the large window curtain, and the tripod, with the head of the Pope wrapped like a mummy, was slid from view.

Pope John and don Giuseppe watched this maneuver with enjoyment.

"Be careful," said the Pope. "If you're seen from the piazza, they'll say we've been reduced to renting studios to sculptors."

"Perhaps we should let him be seen," said don Giuseppe, "to show that five hundred years after the Renaissance, a Pope brings artists back to the Vatican."

"Whatever happened between Popes and artists?" asked Pope John. "Why did the collaboration cease?"

"Perhaps," said don Giuseppe, "because the Renaissance died, and so did its art."

There was, for Manzù, more to it than that, and he was ready to say so if asked. But the Pope dropped the sub-

49

ject, taking him by the arm and saying: "Come, we will go ahead."

They left through the same small corridor, eventually coming to an elevator. It was one of the small ones, the size of a phone booth, which are used in the Vatican. It had a little, fold-down seat and Pope John suggested the sculptor sit on it.

"No, *Santità*, I couldn't do that."

"Please," he said, with a smile and a nod, as though it would indeed give him pleasure.

"Please," he said again, using the Bergamesque form of speech which immediately made it a personal matter. For he had invited a visitor into his home and the elevator was already something of an antechamber. It had a chair and he had offered it to his guest. Manzù was expected to sit down as though they were both two friends from Bergamo. Yet who could sit before a standing Pope? The sculptor shook his head to indicate that it just could not be done.

"No, *grazie*."

This resulted in both men standing, while the seat remained down, further cramping their quarters. Manzù felt lost. His refusal to do as the Pope requested, plus this sudden intimacy—his black suit touching the capacious white papal soutane, the golden pectoral cross hanging a few inches from a blue tie Inge had given him for Christmas—left him further confused and speechless.

As a sculptor, he could easily mold the Pope's big ears, adjust his nose or move an eye in his head. He could prowl over his features and his body as freely as a boy scrambling over sand dunes. But as a man standing beside him in an elevator, he felt helpless. Millions of people would have given anything for this chance to speak intimately to the Pope in Rome—indeed, he had just been praying for the opportunity. Yet now that he had it, he could think of nothing to say.

Finally, as the elevator creaked and groaned upward, John broke the silence, rejoining them to the same human family.

"These old elevators have one virtue . . . they remind you to say your prayers."

"Prayers?" asked Manzù, unsure he had heard right.

John's face clouded slightly at this remark, as with a child when it hears a strange sound.

"Do they break down often?" Manzù asked quickly.

At this, the Pope brightened, brown eyes twinkling.

"Sometimes . . . sufficiently often and sufficiently without serious trouble to prove the power of prayer."

Within a few seconds, his face had clouded and cleared. It had circled from doubt to trust, from defense to delight, turning on the central issue of the validity of prayer which clearly was an orienting point of his life. This was to be expected. He shared it in common with other men and priests. But what appeared most uncommon was his recovery—his grace in overlooking a misplaced question, his pleasure at mending a fractured first bond of trust. This seemed extraordinary to Manzù as did the offer of the elevator seat, because these impulses stemmed from humility—rare enough in most men, but incredible in a Pope.

The door opened and they got off. They were the same height and there was a vague similarity in their features—as though they belonged to the same Bergamasque family. Swiss Guards flashed halberds and clicked heels at their passage through a glass-enclosed loggia and so into the papal apartments—entering first a large reception room. Excepting for some benches, it was bare. On the wall hung a large crucifix, and also a banner of the city of Venice with its golden lion of St. Mark.

"I brought it with me when I came for the Conclave," explained Pope John, looking up at the lion.

"*Venezia . . .*" murmured Manzù.

"*Beata Venezia,*" said John, as though "Blessed Venice" was the official post-office name for the city.

He had left Venice with a roundtrip ticket, telling the people he would be back as soon as the new Pope had been elected. He loved the city and made no secret about it whenever it was mentioned. Yet now, as Pope, he would probably never see it again. So it was *Beata Venezia* with a golden lion hung on the wall of an empty waiting room.

"From there we began our latest journey, which has ended here—carried on high by our children."

"But you expected to return to Venice?"

He paused for a moment, then nodded as though this was important.

"No one is born ready for the place he must occupy. God prepares us through the grace of healthy body and solid roots. Then He measures His assistance according to the new task and the man who must assume it. The secret is to let oneself be carried by the Lord, and to carry Him. Saint Gregory Nazianzen said: '*voluntas tua, pax nostra*— your will, Lord, and our peace.' There's no other explanation to my life, than that."

Manzù looked into the Pope's eyes for some sign that his words were not felt, being more a recitation of old litany on the beauty of obedience, of freedom under the yoke. He saw nothing, however, other than a broad smile and a look in his eyes suggesting that a belief like a light burned within him, forming the central core of his life, and making him strong and vital. Here was a man, he thought, who most certainly was born to be a priest.

Once again the sculptor wondered how someone like this could have been elected Pope. Did the Cardinal electors see this inner light when voting for him in the Sistine Chapel—when Angelo Roncalli was only one of many sitting in a lineup of purple thrones? Or did it break out after he had been dressed in the supreme white and so could allow his true self to finally appear to the world? What miracle allowed him to come to the throne of St. Peter?

They walked on through two smaller rooms, coming finally to his office.

"They call this my private study," said John. "But it's not so private. They find me here as quickly as anywhere else—quicker, in fact, because there's less place to hide."

It had the look of the study of a country lawyer or a threadbare bishop. The walls were covered with red and gold brocade, but otherwise it was quite simple: a couple of tables piled with papers and books, some bookshelves, a white portable typewriter with the Roncalli crest, and an old oak desk with a metal table lamp. Some typed pages and handwritten corrections lay next to an opened book in Latin.

"My homework," explained John, "for the canonization of Saint Gregorio Barbarigo. You know—our bishop from Bergamo."

Manzù had forgotten about Barbarigo. But he understood the Pope's pride and nodded with an odd sense of mutual pleasure. Turning to leave, he noticed a rubber-covered platform beneath the studio window and realized this was where the Pope stood each Sunday when he spoke to crowds in Piazza San Pietro.

"That's the window?"

"Yes . . . my window onto the world."

Chest high off the floor and as wide as two outstretched arms, it was the window where the world saw the Pope. His appearance in it had become a regular Roman event— as regular as the cannon which blasted at noon, from the top of the Gianicolo hill. Invariably, the cannon's boom startled pigeons from their nests in the arms, beards, and hemfolds of stone saints about the piazza, sending them into wild flight around the great dome of St. Peter's, just as the Pope himself appeared in the window—a small, rotund figure in white, waving his arms like a puppet in the sky while the crowd jumped and waved and cried: *"Viva il Papa! Evviva!"*

"Come," said John, stepping up onto the platform. "Come and take a look if you like."

Stepping up with the Pope, Manzu saw the microphones which boomed his voice out to the wild throngs, their coupled coils and massed voltage transforming his gentle, pastor's voice into the thundering of an invisible bull deity chanting the litany of the Angelus and so causing hundreds of believers to drop to their knees upon the piazza's cobblestones:

"In nomine Patris, et Filii, et Spiritus Sancti. Angelus Domini . . ."

After opening this awesome dialogue with God, the Pope always spoke to the people below him in the piazza:

"Miei cari figlioli!"

This direct call to the people, made over the same electrical hookup, invariably had another tone to it—charged with a warm and human quality, as though the Pope was no longer an electronic and angry Jehovah, but rather an imprisoned being, caught somehow on the third floor of the Apostolic Palace.

Other Popes had stood in the same window, saying "My dearest children . . ." but Pope John seemed to say it in a different way. Romans and pilgrims from around the world came to listen and wonder as he asked them variously to drive safely, dress warmly, play fair, love one another and even to pray for a Soviet astronaut. And many came to look at him as though they had lost a father or a brother whom they could find framed in this window every Sunday at noon.

Pope John drew aside the curtain, allowing a view onto

the great piazza where next Sunday's throngs would gather to see him. Now it was practically empty. Formed by the open arms of the Bernini colonnade, it held in its embrace two splashing fountains, a horse-drawn carriage inching around the obelisk, two arguing monsignori walking rapidly toward the shade of the columns, and a herd of schoolgirls with flanking nuns climbing the steps of the basilica.

Beyond this, Rome stretched out in great style. This was truly a window onto the world. From here the Bishop of Rome could survey his parish like a patriarch with a seat in the sky. Each monument, each street seemed close enough to touch with a stretch of the hand. And in the middle lay old River Tiber: a brown rope curving toward the Vatican, then coiling away to the sea.

The pastor and primate of the Roman Catholic Church stood silent for a moment with the sculptor by his side, looking beyond the empty square toward the city and the world

"This view," he said, "never fails to impress and humble me."

"The piazza filled with people?"

"With people who have come, yes—and also those who have not come."

For a brief moment, Manzù prepared for the worst. Don Giuseppe had spoken of him and now the moment had arrived for an instruction and even a warning. The Pope himself was going to do it. That was, he thought, why he had been brought to this apartment.

Yet when Manzù turned to look at the Pope beside him, the thought vanished. The hand with the bishop's ring which had been kissed by uncounted thousands rested upon the stone window sill. His brown eyes continued to search the city, its streets winding over hills and around old forums which once held ancient Rome.

"You see those ruins of the age of the Caesars? Just as they are with us, in our midst, just as the world of Homer

55

and Julius Caesar have not yet died—so the Christian civilization has not yet been completely born."

He continued to look out at the city and the world— *urbi et orbi*—and Manzù felt an exhilarating relief that this very human Pope had not attempted to place a hand upon his life.

"Excuse me, *Santità*, but this birth has been going on for almost two thousand years."

"The fault is our own. We have not yet shown the way. Saint John Chrysostom said Christ left us on this earth in order to become beacons which give light, teachers who give knowledge. He did this so that we may discharge our duty as angels and heralds among men. So that we might be grown men among the young, men of spirit among men of the flesh, and win them over. So that we might be the seed and bring forth many fruits."

He turned to the artist and took his arm, as though this human touch would help convey both his thought and the words of the Greek saint.

"It would be scarcely necessary to expound doctrine if our life were radiant enough. It would not be necessary to use words if our acts were witness enough. If we behaved like true Christians, there would be no pagans."

Manzù nodded agreement. For how could it be otherwise? He recalled his meeting with Pius XII when he was censured by the Holy Office and condemned by a cardinal without even being asked to explain his sculpture. Pagans or non-believers were created every day by such men who called themselves Christians.

The Pope continued to hold onto him.

"As for those who do come into the piazza, my poor person really counts for little. We pray together and we look at one another and we say hello. If they find strength in me, I also find it in them. I will tell you even more: I am a simple brother to them, a brother who became a father by the wishes of our Lord, Jesus Christ. But all of it—father or brother—depends upon God. What we can do that is important is to continue to love one another, to take hold of what unites us, leaving aside those little things which might cause trouble, which might turn us against one another. . . ."

It was as though he was speaking not to the sculptor and fellow countryman, but rather to thousands gathered below in the piazza. Manzù looked down to find some children playing leapfrog over stone pillars. The Pope saw this, too, and smiled broadly. His mouth was especially wide and when he smiled, it stretched almost to the point of caricature.

"The piazza is a playground for many who have no backyard, especially the children. I would like to open the Vatican gardens to them all, so they would have somewhere to hide, to dig tunnels and to play in the woods—instead of the dangerous streets. But it would mean changing some rules around here, and that requires somebody stronger than the Pope!"

There was the sound of voices—don Giuseppe and Monsignor Capovilla approaching. Pope John abruptly descended from the platform, as though he did not yet wish to join them.

"Come," he said. "Come with me."

Manzù followed through the next door and into the bedroom.

Quite clearly, this was his real home in the vast Apostolic Palace. Around the walls were photographs of the Pope's family and he courteously welcomed Manzù into his home by introducing him to them. They went from one photo to another, beginning with John's father who had a mustache bigger than his clumpy black bow tie. Pope

John obviously derived his arched nose, his high forehead and the enormous ears from his father, while his mother had given him her soft eyes and gentle smile.

"We were poor, but it was a good life and we had faith in the future," recalled the Pope. "At our dinner table there was never bread. Just *polenta*, and very rarely any meat. There was no wine for the children or the young people and only at Christmas or Easter did we taste some home-made cake. Clothes and shoes for church had to last for years and were passed from one brother or sister to the other. But, if a beggar knocked at the door, my mother would sit him down at the table with us. Nobody was ever turned from our door."

Pausing before a photo of a church in his hometown, So to il Monte, Pope John said: "Every morning at five the bells would ring out the Angelus and in the next room I would hear my mother saying to my father: 'Get up Battista. The bells . . . *Angelus Domini nuntiavit Mariae* . . .' The prayer would be mumbled all over the house as we children joined in. Then, before going to work in the fields, we'd all troop off together to church for the Holy Mass."

At another photo, he said: "The Franciscan convent at Baccanello. It was over a mile away but we could hear their bells ringing the hours and when they sounded 11 o'clock, my mother would stop whatever she was doing and say: "Time to put on water for the *polenta!*"

A landscape of Sotto il Monte showed the square, block-shaped farmhouses on rolling hills, broken by black cypress against the sky.

"Counting the relatives, we had twenty-eight in our family. Marriage did not mean leaving home, and money went into a common pool. So there was security for every-one—the old, the sick. Even young married couples were helped through the first, hard period when there are mouths that consume and arms that bring in nothing."

Next came photos of his sisters, Ancilla and Maria, each with the same gentle smile—and each one dead.

"Life is something of a boat trip," he said, looking at his sisters. "We say goodbye to those we love, heartbroken and in tears at the separation. But then, when we arrive, others whom we love are there waiting for us on the dock."

There were a number of photos of the young priest Roncalli, his hair crew cut, surrounded by seminary students. Then came one of him some years later, with fellow priests, and another of a group of priests with beards and stovepipe hats whom he explained were Bulgarians with him in retreat.

Finally there was one of Angelo Roncalli with the fat paunch and robes of a bishop, surrounded by four men in ill-fitting Sunday suits and rumpled collars. They all had similar noses and stood erect and unblinking, as though suddenly caught in a private moment.

"My brothers visiting me in Paris when I was Nuncio," explained Pope John. "That's Giuseppino who came to see me when I was Pope and said, 'I can see this is not easy. You are a prisoner of luxury and cannot do all that you would like.' "

His finger touched each of the other brothers: "Zaverio, Alfredo . . . and Giovanni who has departed from us."

He looked back over the pictures of the living and the dead and sighed. "If you think of the time which has past, you can't help but realize you are old. But if you think of the days ahead, you feel younger."

Besides these photos of friends and family, there were statues and images of other friends: saints of the Church and another family, of St. Joseph and Mary, plus various images of the Virgin, including one with Oriental features, and two wooden statues of Peter and Paul. The Pope went on, identifying others dear to his heart: the Madonna of Covadonga, St. Charles Borromeo, St. Francis de Sales, St. Mark the Evangelist, and his beloved Bishop Radini Tedeschi.

Slowly they had worked their way around the room, finally reaching the clothes closet which Pope John opened as though he was also curious to see inside. There were some white papal soutanes, a red shoulder cape, a cloak, and then —on a bottom shelf, two rows of papal slippers. They were red and white and on each one was sewn a golden cross. There was a pair of green ones, too, and all together it made a brilliant array. But it also seemed to leave the Pope uneasy.

"My shoes," he said, and looked at his visitor.

Manzù looked at the shoes and nodded.

"They don't fit as they should," he said.

Manzù nodded.

"They look sort of narrow."

"They are. The best shoes I ever had were in the Italian army. We Roncallis all have big feet and those were just right. You could walk in them for miles and miles and hardly feel it."

"These must be hard to walk in."

"Terrible," he said. But I think it's part of the conspiracy here to prevent me from walking out of the Vatican. Every time I go outside, they get excited as though Italy was too dangerous for a Pope."

There was a tiara in the closet and the Pope took it down. Even for a papal crown, it was very ornate. All three levels were covered with precious stones and encircled with gold and silver bands.

"A gift," he said, "from the good people of Bergamo.

But it's too heavy to wear. Here . . . feel it."

Manzù took the crown into his hands and, indeed, it was quite heavy.

"Porca miseria!" he exclaimed, forgetting he was with the Pope.

John closed his eyes, as though the two words were visible and he did not wish to see them.

"There's no misery here," he said gently, looking at the overweight symbol of his office. "Except perhaps my-self—unable to bear up under what's expected of me!"

Again he had used a pleasant remark to ease obvious embarrassment and so bridge a gap between himself and another human being. He was, thought Manzù, a man with an incredible gift for making everyone feel as though they belonged to one big human family.

"Thank you, *Santità*," he said, handing back the heavy crown.

John looked at it, then at his shoes.

"At my death they will be able only to say of me, as they did of Pius X: 'Born poor, died poor.' Even to my relatives, I can leave little more than a big benediction."

In their tour of the room, they had come at last to his bed—a plain mahogany four-poster. Next to it was a night table with an old-fashioned radio, a call button, and some books, including the Breviary and the Bible. These adjuncts of night and sleep seemed more intimate and personal than anything else in the room. For here the Pope in his night-shirt—without crown or golden slippers or pectoral cross—committed himself to sleep, to dream, and inevitably to die.

"Santità, how many Popes have used this room?"

"Four before me, beginning with Saint Pius X. It was his bedroom during the Conclave and after his election he decided to stay here, rather than move to the floor below

61

where Popes used to live. Benedict XV slept in the next room, but Pius XI and XII slept in this one. And they all died here, except Pius XII who was the first to pass away at Castelgandolfo."

Manzù looked back at the Pope's bed and wondered how it would be to sleep where you knew you were going to die. Modern man moved about so much he could not easily point to his deathbed or even where he would meet death. He had a good chance of dying anywhere, especially in a car—but where, or in what car, he would never know. Yet a Pope could look at his bed and know that it was from there he would most likely leave this earth for whatever awaited him.

Pope John seemed to have understood the sculptor's thoughts. For he nodded with a gentle smile, and turned to gaze at the wall opposite where there was a white crucifix, which could be seen directly by the Pope lying in bed. Beneath the crucifix was a *prie-dieu* where he began each day on his knees, in silent dialogue with God.

Manzù looked up at the ivory figure of Christ and realized this was the only figure in the room which Pope John had not bothered to point out or otherwise describe. Yet why should he? It did not occur to him to do so, any more than a farmer, showing off his land and crops and family, would also point to the sun in the sky. Obviously it was up there, and all life came from it. And so was the crucifix up on high, John regarding it now with an expression of wonderment that another might experience in gazing at the mystery and beauty of a sunset, or spring's first rose, or the act of love.

In that moment Manzù saw what he wanted in order to complete his portrait. It was in John's face and, having seen it, he felt he could realize the work next day: an alignment of features suggesting strength of discipline, obedience, self-denial and love which were the interior components of this extraordinary man.

Don Giuseppe and Monsignor Capovilla entered then, as Pope John said: "So now you have seen how we live. I hope you can come again."

Manzù thanked him and left. On the way out, Monsignor Capovilla said: "The Holy Father sensed you were ill at ease while at work. So he invited you up here to help you relax."

"Tell him that it helped and that I am grateful."

"You'll be ready tomorrow?"

"Yes."

Despite this, Manzù was not ready. He had seen into the Pope, but failed to look into himself. So the second sitting was destined to disaster.

Chapter Six

Don Giuseppe picked up Manzù again for their second encounter with the Pope, and Monsignor Capovilla met them as before inside the Apostolic Palace. On the way into the library, the Pope's secretary recalled a story about a photographer who wanted to do a portrait photo of the Pope raising his hand in the act of benediction.

"At first the Holy Father thought it would be impossible," said Capovilla. "But then he called in an usher and asked if he'd like an Apostolic Blessing. The poor man didn't understand why he was getting such a special favor, but said he'd be happy to have it. So the Pope blessed him, and the photographer got his picture."

Capovilla felt this demonstrated the uniqueness of Pope John. The photographer had asked Pius XII to raise his hand for the same sort of photo — and Pius had done it. But John could not.

"I understand it very well," said don Giuseppe. "It's impossible for him to bless empty air. The act must be directed at some thing or some person, otherwise it cannot exist. It becomes form, empty of meaning. Like a formalized work of art with nothing in it . . . right, Giacomo?"

Manzù agreed, but did not feel like talking about it

now. Form for its own sake was useless, even vulgar — especially in art. A sculptor used form as a means of expression, just as a poet used words. But they were basically instruments to be used toward an end — and not an end in themselves.

"Right, Giacomo?"

"Yes . . . form for its own sake is distasteful."

Pope John was waiting again inside the library doorway and appeared quite pleased to see them. Manzù wore a formal dark suit and tie, as he had the first time. But now John pointed to it with mock displeasure.

"*Eh, beh!*" he said. "You don't plan to stay long, if you come dressed like that."

"Ah, yes . . . these certainly aren't work clothes."

"As soon as you're home, off they come . . . eh?"

Manzù nodded, and John sighed in sympathy.

"I know how you feel," he said, implying they were both prisoners of Vatican dress and ritual. The palace was ruled by a stiff protocol, built around the fixed habits of its occupants — the papal court. Popes came and went, but the court remained forever.

"Well, now that we're alone you can take off your tie and jacket," he said. Then, as if to lead the way, he plumped himself into the chair by the window, quite pleased at the prospect of relaxing and enjoying a good talk with don Giuseppe.

Manzù remained as he was and began to work — noticing immediately that the Pope was wearing his *zucchetto*, or white skull cap, in place of the old-fashioned red *camauro*, with which they had begun the portrait. The sculptor said nothing, however, because he now preferred it this way. The image which interested him, the Pope as he had seen him in his apartment, was with the small skull cap showing the big ears and high forehead. So much the better, he thought, and began to work while John chatted with don Giuseppe about San Carlo Borromeo and other saints.

Almost immediately, however, he ran into trouble. All men in their actions, and especially artists, seek a precise image of their work. Manzù now had one of Pope John. He saw his head in a multiple aspect—as strong, human, and *dolce* — a concept bounded by three themes. But concept is one thing, and doing it is another. Manzù's problem at this point was basic with all artists: sometimes he had the impression he was approaching an image when actually he was going away from it.

Whenever he went too far away, and so felt unable to continue a work, he usually destroyed it and began again. But where it was easy to do this in his own studio, it did not seem possible before the Pope. In one second he could have pulled away the clay face, wadding the nose and eyes and ponderous brow into his fist. But he felt this would astonish the Pope and his attendants and cause general embarrassment—especially for don Giuseppe.

So he worked on and on with the clay, seeking some solution from what he had already made—redoing certain areas in an attempt to recreate the whole. But this was similar to replacing foundation blocks in a house which was already half built. Every movement threatened the entire structure, causing him to hasten from one side to the other as he gradually lost control of the whole.

This was contrary to Manzù's usual procedure which normally had a progressive order, beginning with the basic essentials of the overall column of the head. That is, a lump of clay, fixed on the armature, and shaped roughly like a large lamp bulb. With this before him, the subject is placed at a three-quarter angle, so that the entire face can be seen but with the right half in full exposure. From here the sculptor begins to work, attacking in three-quarter fashion the right side of the face with the first plane created in clay being the one nearest to him—the right cheek bone. After that, he moves onward to successive planes and voids: those of the right eye, brow, lower jowl and temple, and finally the nose.

In this manner, he moves to the left side of the face, working mainly with thumb, forefinger and palm, especially of the left hand—sliding, shifting, lifting, tacking, filling, pulling, padding—all of it happening in one continuous action of hands like feeding birds, wherein he designs and defines without interval.

The movement happens by itself, without thinking about it from the outside, because the artist is in it and it comes by itself. He never thinks of *how* to do a work, but simply of *doing* it. All the problems appear in the moment of action and are satisfied at the same time. Manzù was interested to discover from Picasso that it is the same with him. A work is born and satisfied in one overall action. This can take place in a minute or an hour or longer. If it is a work of heroic size, it can take days or weeks. But it is always part of one cycle that begins and ends, resolving itself as it develops.

Trouble begins when the cycle is broken, or ends without solving all the problems inherent in its growth. When this happens, the artist vacillates from one side to the other, trying to make a whole out of irregular parts—just as Manzù, perspiring in his Sunday suit and tie, was now doing with the head of the Pope.

The difficulty was further complicated by the clay which began to suffer from too much handling. Shakespeare and other poets have described clay as dull and insensate matter. Actually, it is most sensitive. It has grain, as does wood; and, if taken the wrong way, it ruffs up just as wood splinters. Handled too much, it becomes tormented and fractious. Handled quickly, it has a freshness and elasticity. And, after being used and turning hard, it can be reborn again simply by immersing it in water. Indeed, the clay which Manzù used to make this first head of Pope John came from a ballet dancer. At first, it was quite good, but too much handling and reworking had caused it to become a recalcitrant, tormented lump under his hands.

He looked at the work and wondered with growing sadness just where he had gone wrong, and what it was that constantly allowed the image to escape him. Certainly, the surroundings were difficult and against his nature. He was not used to working in a dark blue suit with tie and polished street shoes. He missed the old and battered straw hat he wore when working in his studio. And there was the trouble with his tongue. He had a habit of sticking out his tongue when concentrating, but when this happened before the Pope, he pulled it back, again and again, trying to remember to keep his mouth closed.

These were distracting enough, together with people coming and going and the Pope talking to don Giuseppe. He felt, however, that there was more to it than just this and he tried to discover what it was as he worked the increasingly fractious clay.

Obviously the distractions got through because he was open to them and not closed in on what he wanted to do: the portrait of the bishop of Rome. He had intended to do it with no more personal commitment than would come from a Buddhist or a Hindu or an atheist. The goal was simple and uncomplicated: transfer Pope John's image into clay which would then be fused into bronze for all future generations to look upon as the true likeness of the two hundred sixtieth successor to Saint Peter, Prince of the Apostles.

But he had not been able to do it as quickly as expected. Instead, he had been drawn into the personality of the man and had found it overwhelming. If Pope John were a foreign king or a free-thinking humanist, it would not have been so disturbing. But he was Pope and leader of a church Manzù had left long ago. And now it was as though he was back in a house where once he had lived, wandering through rooms filled with memories of the pain and the joy of departure.

What, wondered Manzù, was he doing there? What had brought him back to look once more at the empty rooms of broken faith? Most certainly, it had not been a mistake to leave—nor was the decision to do so a sudden or impulsive act. It came with a slow accumulation over the years, reaching its crisis in the battle over his naked Christs, nude women and Nazi soldiers which were censured by the Holy Office of the Roman Catholic Church and eventually brought him to stand before Pope Pius XII.

Looking back, even now as he worked on the clay portrait of another Pope, he did not see how he could have done otherwise. He had acted as a creature of his time, an artist who was part of the world around him. And the world, beginning in 1939, became a frightening place with the approach of war's holocaust.

In Fascist Italy it was like being in an automobile, going over 100 miles an hour—only to discover suddenly that the driver had vanished. Manzù remembered that image because it came to him often in his dreams. In another dream, even more terrifying, he entered a theater to see a production of *Medea*. The tragic Greek heroine was already on stage, wearing white robes with swastikas, and killing her children. Only when blood spattered over the footlights onto the audience, did they notice her wild eyes and realize she was actually murdering live children whose screams slowly died. Then, fixed to his seat in horror, Manzù recognized the faces of the children were those of friends who had been taken away by the Fascists.

Inevitably, this affected his art. From 1930 to 1937 he had done three low-reliefs around the figure of Christ— "Christ with Poverty," "Christ with Women" and a "Pietà" —which were fairly traditional in concept.

But as Italy drifted helplessly toward the night of war, he started another series, beginning in the spring of 1939 with "Christ in Our Humanity." The Christ-figure was seen totally nude in the crucifixion, flanked by a fat-bellied Nazi— also naked except for his spiked Teuton helmet with a cross on it — holding a spear to pierce the body above him. A little dog barked, while a nude man and woman prayed and wept at the foot of the cross. It did not matter whether they were Adam and Eve, Joseph and Mary, or anybody. They wept and prayed while the only protesting voice was a barking dog.

There was another one of Christ hanging by one hand while the whore, Mary Magdalena, kissed his hand. She was nude, seen from the rear, and very fat. This obesity caused some to think she was a fat Jewish mother of Christ, and it alarmed those who felt the Virgin Mary had good looks and a nice figure which should be kept under wraps. But Manzù intended it to be Mary Magdalena—or any woman, for that matter. In the same low-relief, two boys playing piggy-back pause to look with the wonder of innocents at the death and sorrow before them.

The next year he did a Deposition, with Christ as a skeleton, witnessed by a naked, pot-bellied old man holding a cardinal's hat. A little boy with a dog stares, not at the forgotten Christ image, but at the flabby old man, as if to ask what he had done to prevent or avenge such horror.

There were eight of these reliefs. It became clear later to Manzù that he had begun to think of Christ as a brother, or a partisan fighter, or one of six million Jews killed by Germans in the ovens and machine-gun pits of Europe—a

holocaust witnessed by the Pope in Rome without pointing a finger or crying out: "Herr Hitler, you must desist
from killing Jews or otherwise treating them as sub-humans,
since God created no such creature!"

Manzù did not intend to become political or create
a scandal. He was simply reacting inside his studio to events
happening on the outside, yet events which were also in
him, carrying him along with them.

When these works were shown in Milan, he was attacked
by the Fascists and the Church as a moral deviate. Cardinal
Costantini, without ever asking Manzù to explain his basic
intentions, called him a scandal monger and the Holy Office
condemned his nudes as "filthy." Nothing helped. Even
the defeat of Fascism and exposure to the shocked world
of the Nazi torture chambers did not alter the official Church
opinion of his nude Christs with Nazi soldiers in the role
of Romans. Finally, a 1947 post-war showing in Rome caused
an even greater outcry. A group of Vatican monsignori
launched a vicious Catholic press campaign against Manzù,
just at the time when he had entered into competition for
the doors of St. Peter's.

At the height of this crisis, he met Monsignor de Luca.
The priest came to a show of his work at the Palma Gallery
in Rome and saw nothing intrinsically wrong.

"You are a primitive Christian—perhaps given to ex-
cess," he said. "But I suspect the Church needs more like you."

"They say I'm a sinner and getting worse every day,"
said Manzù, wondering what could be said to that.

"Well, sinners are needed, too," replied the priest. "Otherwise we wouldn't be able to isolate the saints."

They stood in the middle of the gallery smoking ciga-
rettes, and liked one another immediately. After that, they
began to meet occasionally and one day don Giuseppe sug-

gested Manzù should meet Pius XII. The press campaign had become even more insidious.

"Do you think my seeing the Pope will help?"

"I don't think it will convert your enemies. But it might shut them up for a while."

"That would be something," said Manzù, and agreed to give it a try.

About a week later don Giuseppe phoned to say the audience with Pope Pius had been arranged through the Holy Office.

"It includes your wife and son—and sister, too."

"Why?"

"It will make it less formal, and easier for you."

"I think it would be better to do this alone. It's my business, not my family's."

"They can help by just standing there. Take them along."

Manzù did not want to go that way—a family group, appearing as an example of fidelity to Catholic tradition. But to change the appointment for himself alone would make the situation even stickier. So he agreed to take his son Pio, his wife and his sister Ida.

On the day of the appointment, the little group entered the Apostolic Palace on foot, going through the Bronze Doors, past the Swiss Guards, and up the Scala Regia. Bernini made his noble stairway as if to break or humble the ego of all men. Built with a false perspective, it goes up and up—as though into the sky. Pilgrims climbing its steps feel that God must live upstairs, not a mortal and aging Pope who waits all alone for one final experience of his life: death.

Manzù looked up the steps and thought that here kings and cardinals had trembled in the climbing. Here, too, had come murderers and thieves. And into this same palace also strode Michelangelo—leaving it in fury when Pope Julius kept him waiting.

So they climbed, four of them, and very soon the great stairway had its diminishing effect.

"Giacomo, what are you going to say to the Holy Father?"

"Keep quiet, woman."

"What did he say?" asked Pio.

"He's nervous."

"I'm not nervous and stop jabbering."

No pope or cardinal had ever cowered Michelangelo. Julius II beat him with a stick, but he refused to bend. Paul IV complained about his nudes in the "Last Judgment" and was told: "Tell His Holiness these are mere trifles. Let him first do his job—mend the world—and then we can discuss mending my fresco." And when Biagio da Cesena also complained, Michelangelo put him in hell—in the Last Judgment with a snake around his head. Even Paul III laughed, telling his master of ceremonies: "If the painter had put you in purgatory, I might have done my utmost. But as he has sent you to hell, it is useless to come to me, since from there, as you know, none can be redeemed."

That, thought Manzù, was Michelangelo for you. No Pope broke him. No courtier deflected his stroke. And what the Florentine had told Julius was good enough now for Pius waiting to hear about his naked Christs.

At the top of the stairs they entered the dark, baroque world of the Pope. One great hall led into another, each one containing a different set of Papal courtiers: Palatine Guards, Swiss Guards, Noble Guards, *bussolanti*, secret chamberlains — bright tropical fish in the dark chambers of the old palace, sunk deep in centuries' fathoms.

All along the way, Manzù noted frescoes of naked cherubs, bare-breasted women and nude male torsoes. The house of the Pope was filled with naked creatures. But unlike his creations, these did nothing. They were empty, baroque beings—third and fourth echoes of the first happy holler of Renaissance man. Cherubs fluttered without sweat, breasts heaved without milk or love, and male bodies turned upon themselves and on no one else: silly chambers of neuters pretending to be people.

These were shameful where his nudes were not. For these pretended to be part of life and missed it. They could not deliver nudity's basic promise, because there was nothing to deliver. And where one could expect a source of life, it was turned away or falsely covered with a fig leaf. A leaf on a tree or leaf fallen to the ground is part of the cycle of a year, of a summer, of the taste of fruit. But a leaf over the genitals of a male nude is nothing but dirty underwear and a shameful abuse of nature. Shame was the perversion of promise.

So thought Manzù as he was ushered with his family into the palace, its great halls diminishing in size until they became rooms which tended to angle around one another, as though entering the final recesses of a giant sea shell beyond the reach of tooth or tide. Finally they came to a room with a red and gold baroque throne chair. Here a chamberlain, wearing the ruff and breeches of a Spanish grandee, stood them in one corner. They had finally reached the point within the Apostolic Palace where they would meet His Holiness, the Pope.

"Giacomo. . . ."

It would be, Manzù told himself, a semi-private audience. He would come in, speak a few minutes to us, and then pass on to other waiting groups.

"Giacomo. . . ."

"What?"

"You will kneel and kiss his ring?"

That stairway had worked well on her. So had the diminishing sea shell.

"Giacomo!"

Sweeping into the room toward them, came a pair of Noble Guards, their faces tomato red beneath the gleaming helmets, silver swords swinging next to black boots. Behind this appeared a pair of monsignori with flying purple capes. And then, from within the flying purple, emerged the tall, bone-white figure of the Pope, his hands folded in front and moving as though he were a vertical column pulled on rollers.

Doric, thought Manzù, a Doric column—simple, straight and unadorned in a tangled forest of Corinthian baroque. It came nearer and suddenly his wife and son and sister were on their knees, kissing the ring. He knelt, too, taking the ring hand and seeing below this the slippers, blood red and trimmed with gold. Then he heard the voice of the *maestro da camera*, saying his name.

"The sculptor, Giacomo Manzù . . ."

The tall white column was before him and he looked up to find it topped by blue eyes behind thick glasses, enlarging them into two blue seas fixed on the face of the moon. No other life appeared there, other than those remarkable eyes which seemed as endless as the sky itself. Where did they reach? In their cold depths was there some warm pool, some soft bank for those who searched the world? Then suddenly they vanished—lost behind eyelids like old parchment—only to re-appear and focus directly upon him.

"Ah, yes, the sculptor . . ."

That and nothing more, except the two eyes fixed on him as if to test his courage and ability to navigate across their uncharted seas. Manzù looked back—and said nothing.

Then one of the two monsignori whispered into the Pope's ear. It was, he knew, top secret and most urgent.

For of every form of communication used within the Roman Curia—memo, letter, phone call, encyclical, Papal bull and smoke signal—the whispered word outranks them all. Millions of words are put to paper or sent over wire. But urgent truths and hot gossip go out by whisper, shot anywhere from two inches to one foot from the ear of the listener.

The Pope took his injection from about eight inches, without a blink or a visible sign that he had received anything.

"They have spoken of your work. . . ."

That was what happened to the whispered word. Launched by a recognizable informant less than one foot away, it nevertheless re-emerged as: "*They* have spoken . . ." Manzù realized the audience was not beginning too well. He stood accused of unnamed error by unseen enemies. Against this he was expected to somehow conduct his defense.

"*Santità*, I think there is a misunderstanding about my low-reliefs which has grown out of all proportion. There were eight small ones, in which I sought to show Christ among the men and women of our time. No polemic was intended, either for or against the Church. There was merely a conceptual look at the tragic period of the war."

This brought a slight nod: bare recognition of the explanation. Quite clearly, more was coming.

"There are various ways to present anything. Some of your conceptions, however, were abnormal—if not unorthodox. A skeleton on the Cross and some nude figures needlessly offended sensibilities and caused many people to wonder why you did it."

Why did he do it? *Porca miseria*, what sort of question was that to ask of an artist?

"A work of art is always stamped with its time and in these small compositions my thinking was fixed on their special relationships, and on the terrible tragedy of the war.

77

All else was without theme or concept. And since the liberty to express oneself is a civic right and duty, I never imagined it would offend the Church."

That should have done it—but it didn't. The Pope shook his head as though he had been told an untruth.

"When you exhibited your work, it was not simply a question of personal liberty. Critics were forced to ask if what you saw, naked or otherwise, had sufficient worth or importance to be shown in public and so confuse the faithful . . . as well as shock higher authority."

What did he mean? What higher authority? Was there someone who stood above him—above this primary priest of the total flock?

"*Santità*, it's not that I wanted to show some cardinals nude like Christ. I've always imagined nudity as a sign of poverty—which should not have offended them. As for the others, I never intended that they symbolize Christian authority. I showed them—the Nazi soldiers and generals— because they were killing people with the help of a cult and a power set against the spirit of Christ."

He waited for an answer to that one—but none came. Once again the blue eyes vanished behind parchment, then reappeared to fasten upon him. Where in them was the warmth, the comprehension? And why the cold blink? Was it to wipe out all that he had said? To wash away the twin pillars of his life: his freedom of reason, and the free flight of his working hands?

"Before embarking upon such projects, you should seek spiritual advice. Consultation can save you much anguish."

So the higher authority was not above both of them, but rather above him alone. The sculptor as a man was below everyone in the Church—from priest to Pope. He was expected to take his concept of art to them for spiritual guidance. That meant any priest, or the Pope, would guide his hand.

He felt threatened and, like someone bolting windows and doors against a terrible storm, prepared a defense of the home. His powers and whatever creative talent he possessed belonged to him alone. By giving them to the Pope and allowing him to decide what was art and what was not possible, any artist would become impoverished and forced to beg himself back in little pieces.

They had no right to expect this—that the freedom of creation be taken away, to depend upon the accident of a whispered word in a baroque place. Manzù took a deep breath. Then, with his house barred against the tempest, he opened the front door to ask the Pope to come in. It was his last attempt.

"Men live and work for a living. My work and my person are one thing only. Unfortunately, *Santità*, the work is carried forward by inspiration—and that can't be auditioned beforehand."

He faltered and stopped. It was no use. The Pope, without crossing his threshold, was already making signs of leaving.

"Yes, it's important to work—but the artist must create, not destroy. The Catholic artist especially must foster love and respect for the faith, for the Holy Virgin, for Christ and His servants—and never, never subject them to ridicule. We are sure you know this and we are pleased to hear that you intended no offense."

The hand was offered. Manzù hesitated, then took it with a bow and muttered *"Grazie, Santità."*

There was a rustle of silk and the Pope moved on—once again a Doric column encircled by purple capes and clanking soldiers. The sculptor watched him go with sadness.

A Pope had turned away from the threshold of his home and gone elsewhere. He felt suddenly very lonely and wished that don Giuseppe were there to help him save something, to show how he could be himself—and also be a Catholic.

"Giacomo, it's better now."

"Nothing's better."

"He said he understood you."

"He understood nothing."

"He said he forgave you."

"Yes, if I give him my tools and my clay and sculpt on my knees . . . if he allows me to do that. It's like putting all the chairs straight in church."

"What chairs? He didn't say anything about chairs."

"Let's go, woman. Let's get out of here quickly."

On the way down the Scala Regia, the perspective was reversed and, as the columns and spaces opened up, so did Manzù's spirits until they emerged into the sunny piazza and re-entered the world. He looked around and, blinking in the sunlight, said to himself:

—This is where I belong. Man does not belong to idols or Popes. He belongs to the world. Existence is sharedness. To be is to be with. And being means being with others. Nothing can be defined or created totally apart and alone.

—Behind me, in a dark palace, lives a Pope who does not go into the world. He expects the world to come to him. Quite clearly, I do not belong with that Pope in his palace, nor in his Church.

So he had said and felt on that morning long ago as he walked across the Piazza, never expecting to return. Yet here he was, once again in the same palace. Before him was Pope John, a Pope of another sort. For John went out into the world and quite clearly he felt he was just one more brother on the road—not a saintly ringmaster of a sinful circus.

So where did that leave him—Giacomo Manzù? Had

he been wrong to drop his faith? Galileo had been misunderstood and bullied by a Pope and his court, yet had kept his faith and been proven right. Did this mean that Manzù lacked roots or strength of courage?

Suddenly he felt ill. His head began to spin and he held onto his easel, trying to continue. Yet even as he sought to concentrate on the clay image, his mind turned away. What, he wondered, was the difference between himself and this other man from Bergamo—Pope John?

Most certainly it was in the cradle of their lives. For the neighboring Roncalli and Manzù familes began by facing in opposite directions. Angelo Roncalli's were farmers, within an interlocking caste of relatives who supported all their members. But the Manzù family — or Manzoni as it was then — had its origin in the inner city of Bergamo, without a protective fabric. So it threw the child Giacomo into the world to struggle alone, as an individual, for survival.

For the Roncallis, labor had a meaning. It was an integral part of their lives, linked to the seasons and shaped to the cycle of man's years. But for the Manzonis in the city, labor had already become a commodity beyond their control. Man was not an end in himself. He was only a means to an end—a *finis* which he did not control. Karl Marx had described them, his poor father and his own early life. Their labor was not their own. It belonged to others. You gave it to a factory, to an office—or to a church where you swept out floors, adjusted seats and for a few miserable lire carried the cross in someone else's funeral.

So the Church appeared differently to them. For the Roncallis, rooted in the soil with arms interlocked against disaster from city and sky, the sound of early morning church bells, and those at eleven o'clock when Mamma Roncalli put on the *polenta* water, came as evidence of security and trust and family warmth. But for Giacomo Manzù they rang out with the invading shrill of a factory siren. Or worse, they tolled his private death as a carefree boy bearing a cross at someone else's funeral, his own sorrow obvious before the eyes of other boys and girls who looked coldly at him, knowing he was linked to this one particular death—as he had been to another one the week previous and would be forever—by a skimpy handful of coins, not even enough to buy his part of one decent meal for a family of eleven.

Their separate cradles had launched them—the Pope and the sculptor—onto separate roads, ending in belief and disbelief, all of it depending upon the accident of birth. So the question he had put to don Giuseppe should now be applied to himself: what made him, Giacomo Manzù, certain he was born in the right place, or even at the right time? Nothing. Therefore, his disbelief was also a creature of accident and not of logic. Or was it?

As this conflict raged within him, the sculptor stood back to study his work. With horror, he saw he had created a mask. This was not the man he wanted. It was a mask of a man, with all the lines and folds, as Verrocchio would have done it. He had failed to invest it with the strength and humanity and *dolcezza* of the man sitting on the golden chair, talking to don Giuseppe.

He began to work again. But as he did so, the clay features of the Pope blurred under his hands. He felt the strength go from his arms and legs and he sensed the need to lie down. His head began to spin and he held onto the easel to prevent from falling. The bust suddenly seemed huge—a monstrous cliff with him hanging onto it, a tiny man about to fall.

—*Santo dio* . . . what can I do but hang on and hope for this to pass away? If I faint now, it will be the end of this effort to do the Pope: a dead Alpinist from Bergamo at the foot of a clay mountain.

An Artist and the Pope

—I can hear my enemies speaking of it: "*Manzù? He tried to do a portrait of the Pope and fainted. Fell to the floor, holding clay in his hands as if he thought it was rock. He supposed it could support him up before the Supreme Pontiff of the Holy Roman Catholic Church. Poor fool, hit his head on a chair . . . and they carried him away.*"

—Carried away . . . to where? *Madonna*, where was Inge? How could he get out of here?

He looked around the room, in an effort to steady himself, and found that Pope John saw he was in trouble. Don Giuseppe and Monsignor Capovilla saw it, too, and hurried to his side.

He said it was nothing, but sweat poured down and he was pale and trembling. Monsignor Capovilla hurried up with a glass of water, asking him to sit down. He wanted to rest, but it was impossible. The Pope had risen from his chair and Manzù, recalling them together in the elevator, imagined himself finally sitting in a chair while the Pope stood over him.

"No, *grazie*, I feel better."

"Maybe a cup of coffee or a cognac?"

"No, I'll be fine."

"But we should suspend work until tomorrow—no?"

He nodded agreement and weakly began to cover the work. He had not fallen off the clay cliff. Worse, he was left hanging on to it—until tomorrow.

Chapter Seven

Before Manzù could cover
the clay model with a wet towel, Pope John came to his side,
smiling warmly and showing relief that the sculptor felt
better. Then he began to study his portrait, which seemed a
most gentle act, for it helped everyone overcome an acute
embarrassment.

Manzù looked at him as one does toward an old friend,
then wondered upon what he could base such an assumption. How was it that this man imparted such a sense of
relief by his mere presence? Or even when absent, how could
the thought of his existence have the same effect? At that
moment the Pope came still closer to examine the work,
and the sculptor studied his reactions to it, knowing they
would be important.

Most people approach their first portrait as though
taking a last look at a dead friend. They discover a finality to the cast of their features, as immutable as death itself,
which is the sum total of what they are at that moment in
their life. Generally, they are shocked at this, because they
see much more than they ever allow themselves to witness
in the morning mirror, or in life itself—an experience sus-
tained more by memory and hope than by three-dimensional sight. Confronted with such a total view of naked

self, the ravages of time and passion all too evident on the wild landscape of the face, the mind seeks immediate refuge and flees backward toward an earlier, happier image.

When this happens, the eyes of the viewer stare numbed and unseeing at the object which is too much to be accepted. Gradually, however, the mind regains control. It builds up defenses with secondary images until it no longer needs to look at the one before it. Instead, it sees only what it wishes to see. At that moment, fear and panic fade and the portrait is accepted into the life of the viewer who can never again see it totally. This self-inflicted blindness happens most acutely with vain people.

But not, Manzù noted, with Pope John. He looked at his image as if absorbing it with all his senses. There was the unguarded, open approach of a child whose mind has not been conditioned by school and society to snap open at the known and to narrow down before the unknown. And like a child, or any primitive, he was instinctively tactile. Noticing how large the sculptor had made his ears, he lifted a hand—his right one, with the ruby-red ring— to check the enormity of an ear and its thick, pendant lobes.

At this, he smiled again and his eyes had the twinkle of one suddenly meeting some old friends at a bend in the road. He turned then to Manzù with a nod which seemed to indicate they had not seen each other for a long time and had a great deal to talk about.

"How extraordinary is the artist's hand which can create a living work!"

"This is still far from life, *Santità*."

"Yet you want to make it so. And since God is perfection, you seek something divine. It would seem this pursuit can only have an ennobling effect upon the soul."

"Quite honestly, *Santità*, the effect is also confusing."

"Yes, but there are confusions in any search. What matters is that you seek. Also that you love humanity. Otherwise you wouldn't spend a lifetime creating it with your hands and your heart."

What was there to say to this? Manzù mumbled his thanks and felt an immense relief. John had come outside his Church to say that it was not built of bricks and mortar but rather of men and women, and what held it together was love. If he was ready to do this—to come outside and stand with him, with his disbelief and his refusal to enter— Manzù felt ready to meet the Pope any day at the door of his Church. Within him, a massive lock suddenly opened. They had found a common meeting ground where the issue of belief and disbelief no longer separated them, or their families.

"Shall we meet again tomorrow?"

"*Sì, Santità.*"

The Pope looked back at the clay model of himself.

"You mustn't worry if you think it is not going too well, because you can always come here. Come and we will talk a little. It's a pleasure for me. If this doesn't resolve itself today, it will tomorrow. Or it will next month. So remain calm."

He smiled again, touching the artist's arm, as was his habit when seeking close human contact. Then he left, followed by Monsignor Capovilla.

Manzù started to wrap the wet towel and cellophane around the clay, but stopped—seeing suddenly where he had gone wrong. Quickly, he began to make a few changes while don Giuseppe hovered anxiously over him.

"It *looks* like him," said don Giuseppe, trying to be helpful. Manzù wished the priest would shut up or even go away and let him work in peace. But don Giuseppe's face was too full of concern and sadness for him to do other than answer him.

"That's the trouble," he said. "It *looks* like him, but it isn't. It misses. It's a mask. It's not the man inside—only his outside."

Capovilla returned, anxious about Manzù. The sculptor assured him he felt much better and began to cover his work.

"Do you know what the Holy Father said to me just now?"

"No."

"He said, 'I'm happy that you also like Manzù.'"

Manzù stammered some words of gratitude and, after putting the work behind the curtain, left with don Giuseppe.

"Why does he like me?" he asked.

They had driven out through the Gate of the Bell and now, within the high enclave of stone saints atop the encircling Bernini colonnade, were crossing Piazza San Pietro.

"Why?" he asked again.

"Perhaps because you are yourself and nobody else, which is unusual for him. You must never forget that when a Pope is elected, he loses all his friends, even his family. He lives alone, in that big palace you have seen, with an army of guards and priests who call themselves his pontifical family. But they are really strangers who will bury him when he dies and at once get ready to elect another Pope. That's his world, where he lives—the so-called father of everyone, yet without a friend to call his own. Most men weep when elected Pope, and it's not surprising. It's the loneliest job in the world—next, of course, to being an artist."

Manzù smiled, but shook his head.

"I'm lonely only when I can't work and it must be the same for John. I doubt he's lonely, since his belief is the central axis to his life and he turns about it all the time. No . . . we are not two lonely people."

"I was thinking of the pleasure of friendship, Giacomo. Each man can use it—even a Pope. Especially if the friends are worth it."

"You see? We're back to where we started—why does he find me worth his company?"

"As I said, you are you and nobody else. He can trust you to be what you appear to be. Also, you have common roots. You're from the same area, he knew your father, and you speak the same dialect. It's as if you came from the same household."

"We had different cradles."

"Really? I'd say it was the same one, only you both stepped out from opposite sides. And now . . ."

Don Giuseppe smiled and nodded as though hearing voices. It was a habit of his, and a sign to be careful—for it meant he was preparing one of his dialectical traps. They were formidable operations, suddenly yawning open in the middle of an argument, like a jungle pitfall. They could swallow anything from an elephant to a Jesuit.

"As pastor and priest, the Pope is interested in why you emerged from your side of the cradle, just as you are interested in why he went his way—right?"

The trap, at first glance, seemed fairly obvious to Manzù. It lay in the concept of a single cradle and also that the Pope and he, as children, had possessed a freedom of choice and so took separate roads. If he agreed to this, then he had to admit that one of them began life consciously going with the grace of God—while the other denied His grace, and even His existence. But this was not so, since they were the products of separate cradles and separate worlds they never made.

The Pope, as a child, was awakened by the sound of Angelus bells and a houseful of children and parents mumbling their prayers. Each day, before bending over in the fields, he could sit upright and reflect in church. It was a place of retreat, of quiet thought, of search for himself—perhaps even a haven from the bone-ache monotony of farm life. So the entry into church had a special, precious mean-

89

ing in the cycle of his life, as did the seasons to the seeded fields. Such was the world waiting for Angelo Roncalli when he stepped from his cradle.

But it was not the world of Giacomo Manzù. He did not choose to carry a cross at a stranger's funeral. He had to do it to obtain bread, as did his brothers and sisters. Nor did he ask that his hours in church be spent lining up chairs like bowling pins. If there had been bread, perhaps there would have been time and chance to wonder about the mystery of the Holy Cross, perhaps even to love it. But there was no mystery, other than how to cling to life, his hands freezing as he bore the Cross to the cemetery in the winter, his eyes avoiding those of school companions, his heart asking questions of God which brought no answer—questions he later asked in bronze, causing the Pope in Rome to shake his head.

"No, don Giuseppe, we took different roads because we came from different worlds that shaped us and sent us separate ways."

"But why did yours, going toward art, take you away from the Church?"

"I didn't go *toward* art. I found myself *in* it—sculptor by a necessity as natural as eating or sleeping. The religious education came from my parents who insisted upon it as a precise obligation because it dealt with saving or condemning our life after death. I'm not an enemy of the Church or of the bishops and cardinals, but I'm convinced that their hierarchy is far from the spirit of man today—if there's any contact at all with the people, with workers and farmers and those with whom I feel most close. You're a priest, but you're my dearest friend because you're not a professional cleric or bent on a career. You're a man of learning and you'd open up to anyone—as you've done for me."

They were silent for a moment. Along the Tiber, the

plane trees had put out fresh leaves of a bright green and through them the sun shone now, making a yellow and green pattern. Below this, flanked by cars and buzzing motor-scooters, they raced through dark, dappling shadows. When don Giuseppe spoke, he looked ahead toward the sun and the shadows.

"Thank you, Giacomo. I hold your friendship close to me."

"You know how I feel about this."

"Yes, and you must tell this to the Holy Father."

"Why should I? Why should what I think interest him?"

"Look at it this way, Giacomo. You are head of a world church and your biggest single threat is indifference and disbelief. Millions of Catholics no longer go to church, while millions of others have ceased to believe God exists. Suddenly you meet a man from your countryside, an artist of great talent, of unquestioned honesty, and a man who, like millions of others, no longer believes in the Church or God. He speaks your dialect, you trust him, and you must sit before him for a portrait. Wouldn't you accept his talk and company with some interest?"

"You give me too much importance. What can I tell him which he does not already know?"

"He needs to constantly develop on what he already knows. Knowledge, like truth or liberty, must be continually built upon. Otherwise it loses its relevance and becomes weak and meaningless to everyone except scholars."

That was true enough, thought Manzù. But it did not make sense that a Pope would seek to extend his knowledge of disbelief through someone like himself. He looked at don Giuseppe waiting for a reply with the quizzical look of an owl.

"No, don Giuseppe, I'm neither scholar nor specialist in this sort of talk."

"You're an artist and that's a highly sensitive instrument, no?"

"The Pope doesn't need instruments. He has blind faith."

"That's not enough for a Pope nor for an artist, nor for any leader or creative person. Each has his own personal compass. It swings on instinct and it is read by an inner eye. Those who have it seem to be flying blind, on faith alone, and this frightens some people. But it isn't so. Pope John's call for a Vatican Council, for example, was a great flight involving millions of people—indeed the whole Church. It required courage, faith and a sense of direction which not everyone possesses. In fact, when he told his cardinals what he was doing, they sat speechless before him. No one dared to say it was a great idea—until later, when it was considered safer to do this than to remain quiet."

What did John do, Manzù wondered, when his cardinals sat before him in silence without the courage to speak about so great a dream? Did he look for an answer in their faces? Or did he turn away from them to look at a nearby crucifix? Most certainly, it was a moment in which he felt the weight of the papacy and why he alone had been elected.

Don Giuseppe turned from his driving to look at Manzù through thick and dusty glasses.

"The goal of his flight—that is, the aim of the Council—includes embracing the separated brother, the unbeliever, and that's you, Giacomo. You know more about the cause of your disbelief than his professional advisers. So John would instinctively turn to you."

"Until now, he's asked me nothing like that."

"He won't. Not directly, anyway."

"Then what will he ask?"

"I don't know. But he will obtain what he wants without embarrassing you. For, to do so, would be against his nature."

Beneath the trees, the car raced on through more pools

of shadow and sunlight, emerging suddenly onto the Palatine Bridge. Below them, the Tiberine Island sat in the middle of the Tiber, white stone splitting red waters of the river. Two boats lay upside down on its bank, like a pair of fat women, and next to them stood a young man kissing a girl.

Movement was the cause of all life, as Leonardo had noted, but it also had to be directed toward some one thing— toward an accepting sea or waiting clay. Without this, there was stagnation or spillage, and the anarchy of death's rot. Death was ugly because it went nowhere. Life was desirable because it did—or, at least, promised to do so.

He thought of Inge—of the soft curve of her shoulders, her face and her body. At home he would begin to work on a figure of her as a dancer adjusting her hair, her hands above her head, making it long and tense. The title did not matter. Art was an invented world and a true work of art had no theme—only dream-like inspiration. Where the dream ended, reality began; but where reality began, art ended. And the dream was what was lacked in the clay bust hidden behind the curtain in the library of Pope John.

Chapter Eight

THE next day the Pope called him "Giacomo" for the first time, speaking in dialect, as though they had met on a country road near Sotto il Monte:

"*Coma stèt*, Giacomo?"

"*Mè sto bè, e Lü?*"

"Good, good," he said, happily.

Manzù was further surprised to learn from Capovilla that the Pope had prayed for him that morning—a most moving gesture, he thought, but wasted on someone like himself. The whole believing world dwelt under the umbrella of the Pope's daily prayers, while he lived elsewhere without such thoughts.

Yet he did feel better. He continued to dislike the surroundings and the way he had to labor. But there was a growing sense of affection between himself and the Pope which eased the tension and gave him confidence. Unwrapping the work, he no longer had the sense of clinging to a clay cliff. The mask was still there, but so were signs of life. Seizing upon these, he began to work quickly and well, while don Giuseppe and the Pope embarked upon another lengthy discussion of saints and theology which was soon lost upon his ears.

As one drifting away from a shoreline, Manzù separated

from all sense of being in the room or even of being himself. He became an instrument of transference, totally obedient to all his senses, every muscle and fiber moving as though weight and fatigue no longer had claim upon him. He was locked in with his work.

It was an experience he knew well, bringing with it a sense of moving weightlessly off into another self, a separate state of being—borne above earth, beyond reach of gravity and of all moral and social ties to mankind. The flight itself was effortless, as in a dream where one moves soundlessly over great spaces. There was a sense of rising without ever looking back, all of him engaged in the flight, toward the new presence. And with it went the total, unquestioned immolation of self upon a canvas, a lump of clay, or a rock, just as it would be, no doubt, with others creating a rocket or a song or a chemical which never before existed in a raindrop or in the brain of man.

"Is a mask worth anything, Giacomo?"

At the sound of his name, Manzù looked up to find both Pope John and don Giuseppe waiting for an answer.

"Excuse me?"

"Is the mask of a saint or a Pope or a poet, such as Dante, acceptable as a portrait?"

"The mask?"

"Yes, the death mask. We were discussing the features of Saint Barbarigo as seen in a mask taken after his death."

"Ah, it has no value, other than a mask, such as the mask of Freud or Einstein or Marx. They are only masks."

"But they are the exact features of the person," said don Giuseppe, "as if he had just fallen asleep."

"No, because beneath the skin of a living person there is something that runs, and when they are dead, there's nothing running. It's a dry leaf."

"And this change, how long does it take?"

"Immediately, instantly."

Both men thought about this for a moment. Don Giuseppe spoke first.

"St. Augustine says 'man is a soul who makes use of a body.'"

The Pope said nothing. He seemed to be reflecting on how this could happen so quickly. How could the departure of the spirit immediately alter the shape of its former residence? Was the soul a departing wind, an escaping pneuma, immediately deflating its old container? A shadow of sorrow crossed his eyes, as though seeing the lifeless form of someone he loved. Then it passed away, and he turned to Manzù with a slight smile.

"So, only the mask of a living person can be used for a portrait?"

"No, *Santo Padre*, not even that."

"No? And why not?"

"Because the work of even the smallest artist is never based on reproduction. The drive, even if it fails, is never toward imitation, but rather to invent, to create . . . and thus to alter. That applies also to portrait work."

"So you seek to show in your work the interior qualities of a person as they are reflected on the surface at one or another moment?"

"Look, *Santità*, regardless of my role in it, I've always considered art to be an invented world. Without dreams, the continual metamorphosis of art cannot be understood. For instance, a bust of you done by three great masters such as Michelangelo, Raphael and Leonardo would result in three portraits, each different from the other. The same thing would happen if you chose three modern masters. Matisse, Braque and Picasso would give three different versions of yourself. This shows that the dominating element, even with portraits, is the personality of the artist. And in a good portrait you discover something of the subject and also of the man doing it."

97

The Pope thought a moment, then shook his head.

"The argument of art is something which in my life has never formed part of my studies. I go as far as I can—humanly. And from what I understand, a portrait should be precise, that is, it should resemble the features of the person being represented—no?"

He obviously wanted to understand this and Manzù sought some way of making it clear to him.

"Let's take, for example, a bust of Julius Caesar."

The Pope nodded.

"History has given us many busts and statues of Caesar. From the hair, the nose, the mouth, and from the general overall appearance, you can see it's more or less the same person. Yet how many interpretations, and most of them really different portraits—which proves, I think, what I was saying."

He paused, and the Pope nodded again to continue.

"My conscience as a sculptor tells me that certain roads are obligatory. I find them, through experience and ideals of work, just as I find this clay now in my hands. For me, a good portrait does not mean making a copy or being faithful to the outward appearance of the subject. As now with us, it means to think, first of all, of the significance of the portrait, of the personality which basically dominates all and everything—and also of how best to do the work."

The Pope looked at Manzù with such warmth and affection, his face soft with a smile of comprehension, that the sculptor was overcome and glanced down at the clay in his hands. Then he heard John say: "Yes, yes—of course, you must do a portrait which satisfies you. You must follow your conscience all the way. This must come before all else."

Manzù looked up and their eyes met. At that moment he wanted to say: "Thank you, thank you, Papa Giovanni, for understanding the principles of my work and my life. Thank you for allowing me my measure of dignity. Thank you for being Pope. We have waited for you for a long time, so long no one ever expected it to happen in our lifetime."

But he could not say it. He could only hope the Pope understood, as he mumbled his thanks.

"*Grazie, Santità, grazie.*"

Turning back to his work, he thought how beautiful it was to meet with this man who lived in contemplation and reflected each day on the basic good inherent in all men. The pure priesthood was a central condition of his life. He turned on that axis, and the spirit which it generated illuminated his actions as much as reason itself, charging the past, the present and the future.

With a shock, Manzù realized this was substantially the definition of an artist's life, which he had often taught his students—that art must be the central condition of their lives, and never marginal, for the spirit was itself a guiding force in life, just as was reason, and would always remain so.

He looked at the Pope, chatting with don Giuseppe, and realized that their differences turned on two types of faith—his in aesthetics, John's in God. Yet for both of them, faith was a means of defense, to be realized through continual application of self in work, in solitude and in contemplation. John was the drama of man seeking the substance of God, while his was that of man seeking, through the spirit, the substance of life. If God was infinite beauty, certainly infinite beauty could be Godlike. And if there was a ladder of love leaning skyward, there was one of beauty, too. Their souls, if they ever met, would most certainly lean on one another.

With these, and similar thoughts, Manzù continued to work while enveloped by a strange sense of euphoria.

Finally some friends of the Pope were admitted into the library by Monsignor Capovilla. A photographer came, too, insensately shoving the cold, unblinking eye of his machine into the nimbus of Manzù's thought and work.

He did little more that day. The bust was almost finished, except for some final touches to be done in his studio. It did not satisfy him, however, and he decided to do another one. So when the Pope proposed they meet again later in the week, he readily agreed.

Chapter Nine

A<small>T</small> their fourth encounter three days later, Manzù began working in a new clay form and the Pope noticed it immediately.

"A new one, eh?"

"*Sì, Santità.*"

"The other doesn't please you?"

"Not completely, *Santità.*"

"*Va bene,*" he said, sitting down again in the golden chair, as though about to begin a train ride. Indeed, it was only the beginning of a long trip for both of them. Later Manzù wondered if the Pope was aware of it at the time.

John began to talk about little villages near Sotto il Monte and especially of Calusco which had a lovely church and was a happy town. He spoke a bit about the village priest and the men and women he had known there.

"Who knows," he said, "what they would do in Calusco if they knew you were doing a portrait of me? Perhaps if you were to go there, they would make an arch of flowers for your arrival."

Manzù imagined himself going under an arch of flowers surrounded by waving and cheering townsfolk, and shuddered at the thought. It was better to be clean inside and a disgrace outside. Leonardo was right when he said,

"We grow in reputation like bread in the hands of children."
Fame was a sleeping pill and hunger was the stalking companion of champions.

He said nothing, however, and the Pope continued to reminisce with don Giuseppe about other villages and old friends he had known. One story led to another and after a while Manzù had the impression they came from the Bible and not from the early life of a farmer's son. Then he realized that in a certain way this was true. For the Biblical intelligence of Pope John's mind led him constantly to see the workings of God in his own life through these encounters with people, especially those of his childhood who were bound together in a Christian community. His were happy wanderings through countryside where the Christian habit of life was upheld by living tradition, where calloused hands were used in love and prayer and where songs were those of God and the people.

After a bit, the Pope turned to Manzù and said: "Do you like to walk, too?"

"*Sì, Santita.*"

"We used to walk everywhere," he said. "To school, to church, to the fields, to the mountains. I was a swift runner, too. I ran most of the five miles to school and back. In Rome sixty years ago, I could make it from the center of the city to Monte Sacro or the Tre Fontane faster than any of my companions. Then they put me in the infantry and there we walked all day and all night."

They were silent for a while, then he continued.

"I still like to walk, but now I'm forced to go by car and so I'm getting out of practice. When I was Nuncio in Paris, I enjoyed walking about the streets when it was possible, but the Pope heard about it and asked me to stay home, or go by car. And now that I am the Pope, it's no easier.

Here in the Vatican, they don't like their bishop to walk anywhere, except in the back garden where they can keep an eye on him like a prisoner."

Manzù replied that he loved strolling around Paris, too, but London even more.

"London has magnificent parks," said the Pope.

"And great museums, with the Elgin marbles," said don Giuseppe.

"Also St. Paul's cathedral," added the Pope. "What an architectural inspiration!"

His admiration for the great cathedral reminded Manzù of an event during a visit to London to attend an exhibition of his sculpture.

"Recently I was in London with my brother-in-law, Mario Zappettini, who is very religious. During a walk, we came upon a church and I said, 'There's a church for you, Mario.' But he looked at it with suspicion, saying: 'There are two dogs in front of it. It must not be a church of our faith.' I also saw two large marble dogs on the steps, but I didn't believe it meant one thing or another. So I told him: 'Go on in, Mario. It's probably a church for hunters.'"

The Pope burst into laughter and Manzù continued.

"So we went inside. It was a beautiful church. But Zappettini didn't make the sign of the cross, nor did he genuflect or do anything else, and when we came out he said it was not a Catholic Church."

Pope John shook his head.

"It's all the same," he said. "One church is like all others. Two dogs out in front doesn't make any difference, if God is inside."

"Animals and birds creep and fly all over Catholic churches," said don Giuseppe. "Dragons, dogs, cocks, snakes, lions . . . why would two dogs be suspect?"

Manzù agreed with don Giuseppe. Dogs ran, barked and scratched themselves all through Christian art. St. Jerome, for instance, was inseparable from his little white terrier.

Again they were silent. Then the Pope spoke.

"We have to begin by not frightening people away with dogs or lions or theology. We must remove what divides us. It is up to us ordinary Christians to not fear dogs or differences but rather open our church doors as we open our arms to one another."

"Maybe you saw a pair of lions and the church was dedicated to St. Mark," suggested don Guiseppe.

"No," said Manzù. "They were plain dogs."

"In religious art," said don Giuseppe, "the lion is sometimes St. Mark and at other times it is John the Baptist crying in the wilderness like a desert lion. But in the Apocalypse with the four beasts guarding the Lord's throne, St. Mark is the lion, St. John the eagle, Luke the ox and Matthew the beast with the human head because his gospel begins with Our Lord's ancestry."

"Of all the lions of Venice," said the Pope, "the two most useful are those in the Piazzetta. Besides guarding the archbishop's house and the basilica, they also serve the children of Venice as rocking horses."

"St. Theodore is in the piazza, too," said don Giuseppe, "standing on top of a crocodile, though I've never understood why he is standing on it."

There was no answer to this and Pope John said: "The lion is often revealed as a good friend of the saints. Two of them are said to have helped St. Anthony bury St. Paul the Hermit."

"Who lived 115 years in the wilderness," added don Giuseppe, "and during the last 69 was fed by a raven. What wonderful legends! They remind us how once man sought to live in harmony with nature—before Descartes and the industrial revolution separated them. So from Giotto's St. Francis talking to the birds, we come to Brancusi's 'Bird in Flight' —a great work, a captured arc of flashing flight, but sadly without man or any relationship to him."

Manzù felt don Giuseppe was wrong on this one. Man was there, *inside* Brancusi's bird, blasting himself off into space. But before he could suggest this, Pope John said:

"How is your work on the great doors for St. Peter's going?"

Ah, he thought, so the question has finally come. He had been waiting for it and now it was before them and there was nothing else to do but tell the truth.

"He plans a series of animals along the bottom of the doors, *Santità*," said don Giuseppe, trying to soften whatever was now about to happen.

"So it is going well?" asked the Pope again.

"No, it is not, *Santità*."

"And why not?"

"Because they die in my hands."

"What dies—the doors?"

Manzù nodded.

"Why do they die? Don't you feel right doing them?"

They had come immediately to the point. It happened so quickly that Manzù did not know what to say. Getting no reply, the Pope took another tack.

"Why don't artists today feel these things? Why is there this wall between us? Once there was a great river of religious art flowing through the Church."

He had asked this same question when they first met and here it was again. Manzù recalled what don Giuseppe had said in the car, that the Pope expected to hear the truth from him. And now the priest stood beside the seated Pontiff, waiting for him to say it. Clearly, he was expected to speak

107

frankly and to express exactly how he felt about these things. So he began with what he considered to be the basic problem.

"*Santità*, if you will permit me, religious themes don't exist any longer in contemporary art. Today's masters don't handle the subject, either in painting or sculpture. I think that is because religion no longer is the center of a man's life, just as the Church is no longer the home and refuge of his spiritual or psychic self. Once, religion had a power and a reality touching Dante and Michelangelo and others. At that time, dogmas, rites, symbols and images had real meaning for man and so, as a result, did religious art which figured them. But today the images no longer speak the same way because life is elsewhere in science and the industrial revolution which has changed the world."

The Pope sat silent, waiting for him to continue. Don Giuseppe, suddenly concerned about where this was taking them, tried to redirect the talk.

"Surely, Giacomo, you are putting too much emphasis on image. Images, even those of the Church, are constantly altered to fit their time. Every natural thing or event tends to become a sign of something else so that all of nature is destined to be a broad symbolism or language by which God informs us of his plans."

"I didn't intend to say that your images don't represent God. I'm only saying that faith in God is no longer at the center of the thinking of contemporary man because he no longer believes in immortality and doesn't see how his own morality can follow that of the Church."

"So what can he believe in?"

"Man himself, and the road he must take because man is history's main protagonist. The road he travels is no longer that of legends, miracles and sermons. Man today lives with his history and his hopes which he produces with his own hands. And he gives this the emotions he once gave to religion."

"Are you saying science is replacing God?"

"No, I'm not saying anything so definite or immense. I'm already embarrassed at saying as much as I have. But, *Santità*, if you will allow me once more, I didn't say that man, with the atom and other miracles of science, was on the track of solving all his problems—only that this has become the challenging frontier which gives him the strength to go ahead—alone, by himself."

"Why do you say he goes alone?"

"Not wholly alone. To serve someone makes sense, but to serve yourself alone—what misery. No, I intended to say that man must go it alone—or better, that all decisions depend on him and all is within his reach. From love to culture to all other human experiences, he can aspire to the Muses of art and science and humanity, making them the reflective chapels of the inner man—man who constantly seeks more, telling himself: 'Life is not there, where there is nothing to change.' So everything today depends upon man, without his having the time or intention of occupying himself with problems of faith."

He had spoken, perhaps too much, but this was the substance of himself and his work and he had been asked to say it to a man whom he admired above all others. So it was impossible to redirect the thrust. Yet having spoken, he looked at the Pope with sudden fear that he had gone too far before such a sovereign figure.

If so, John did not show it. He nodded he understood and, for a moment, smoothed his cassock flat over his knees. Then he said: "I do not fear for the habits, the politics, or the religion of any man anywhere in the world as long as he lives with an awe of God."

This, thought Manzù, was a humanist concept beautiful and unexpected from a Roman Pope.

"But what you are saying," he continued, "is that this sense of awe is going, or is gone, and that man lives to serve himself alone. If so, then this is indeed very grave."

Since this was not exactly what Manzù had intended, he hastened to explain further.

"Pardon me, *Santità*, I wanted to say that those two inches of poetry which a man carries within him are at the service of no one today—no sovereign, no temporal or spiritual power. I don't mean, however, that they should be an end in themselves, but rather reach out to the benefit of everyone, and that every Muse remain in place and speak with its own tongue."

The Pope replied to this at once: "Then I think it's better for you, with the Muses in place, to finish the doors for St. Peter's immediately. After that, we will see what our Lord has to say."

Manzù heard the Pope but did not immediately realize the implications—that this was not one more link in their talk. It was, instead, its resolution. It was the end—and an unexpected beginning. He looked up to see John's warm, brown eyes, his broad smile, waiting for a reply.

"Finish them for me—can you do that?"

"*Sì, Santità*, I will do it."

He heard himself saying it, as one hears his own voice on a tape, and recognized it with fright. What had he said? He was a servant of no one—no sovereign, no Pope, no man. He was the slave of his work and his work was encompassed by belief. Yet this belief did not include a pair of doors for St. Peter's, attesting that Heaven was a private preserve for Christian glory.

He could not participate in such a work. Yet he had now promised to do it for the man before him. He had given his promise as to a friend and to a man one could love and respect. Yet this did not alter the doors, nor that someone other than John, the man, now held his promise. This was the Supreme Pontiff of the Holy Roman Catholic Church, the Vicar of Christ on earth—and to him Giacomo Manzù owed no bond.

Confused, he looked toward don Giuseppe and found him staring back with open concern. The priest knew what a big leap had been taken. He knew what an abyss of despair lay ahead. And because of this, it was don Giuseppe who suggested calling a halt to the sitting. Later, Manzù could recall nothing else—except that he could work no more that day and so hastily took his leave.

111

Chapter Ten

Don Giuseppe accompan-
ied Manzù down to the Court of San Damaso where a
Vatican car was waiting to take him home. The priest had
an appointment and could not leave, but promised to phone
as soon as possible. They had left the dark palace and, in the
blinding sunlight of the courtyard, stood squinting at one another. Don Giuseppe was obviously worried.

"Where will you be?" he asked.

"I don't know."

"I'll call you at home."

Manzù nodded.

"We can work this out, so stay calm."

Another nod.

"Don't worry," he said.

But the sculptor did worry all the way home and Inge
saw it as soon as he entered. She was in the kitchen with
the maid and the egg man, looking at some pecorino cheese.
When she saw Manzù, she put the cheese down and together
they went into the living room.

"What happened, Giacomo?"

"I want to get out of town."

"Out of town—where?"

"Anywhere. To the beach. I need air."

113

"Don't you want to change your clothes first?"

He shook his head.

"But what is wrong, Giacomo?"

"I promised to finish the doors."

There was more to it than this and she felt it. So he told her:

"I promised it to the Pope."

Inge said no more. Their bond, which began with silent looks, had grown with them. They did not need many words, especially in moments such as this one, which had all the alternatives of a train wreck.

With Inge driving, they started for the beach. Manzù did little more than watch people in the street and in other cars, mostly children whose frank and searching eyes somehow made him feel better. Near Ponte Marconi, he saw a bride weeping in the back seat of a limousine moving alongside them. Her face was wet with tears, and she had the dark eyes and rich lips of Michelangelo's nymphet Eve—the slender, childlike one which nestles under God's arm in the Sistine chapel, staring with wonder at the nude Adam below her, the first man made of flesh and hunger. In the next fresco, depicting her carnal birth, Eve has been taken from the arm of her God Father and consigned to Adam, for she is seen emerging from his rib—the first of the Judaic-Christian virgin births and a passage which forever encased her in man's flesh. But before that happens, she is a slender nymphet Eve and there is a child's wonder to her eyes, just as there was in those of this beauty sitting barely four yards away from him as they raced toward the sea at sixty miles an hour.

Next to her sat an old man, dressed for the wedding, with a white carnation in his lapel. He seemed quite embarrassed beside such grief and stared straight ahead at the chauffeur's neck. Was this old, unbending reed her father? Or was it her bridegroom, her withered and yellow Adam who would bring her tiny packages of horror by night and great floods of shame by day?

They paused at a traffic light and, as a boat moves slowly about in the tide, she turned her glance toward Manzù. For a moment they stared at one another—her dark tear-filled eyes seeking his while his own sought to plunge totally into hers. They remained that way, as two people locked in embrace, until the cars began to move. Then he smiled at her and she opened a little smile in return. With that, they lost sight of one another.

Some people needed a tug at the cassock, or a speaking father, or a smile at a traffic light for the courage to go ahead. But others needed it for the courage to stop, to get off the track, to say no to love's failure, to say *Basta* to the dead myth—and yes!—to lay down the tools and say: "I will not do it. Some of me must be in my work. The human being who produces must also feel."

"Yes," he said. "It's enough."

"What?" asked Inge, slowing down.

"I can't do the doors," he replied, "because I can't cut myself in half."

They turned onto the Via Laurentina which winds through a rolling landscape of green fields and grape orchards—coming finally to Tor San Lorenzo, where they went to sit on the beach and look out at the sea.

He had hoped for some relief and it came almost immediately. The waves seemed to rise up and hang for a moment like green bells—where had he heard that before?—while the sun sat low in the sky, its rays slanting through a few clouds, before finally fusing into the sea and the sand around him. It was just the kind of enveloping canopy of earth, sky and water which he had wanted to find. Beneath it all, he sank back as would an exhausted swimmer who, bare-

115

ly reaching the beach, falls spent upon its shoreline. With his back upon the sand and the sky above, he breathed deeply and let himself drift. In a few hours, he would have to rise up and wrestle the world—the world that had enmeshed him with the doors of St. Peter's. But for the moment, it was enough to breathe and feel life returning.

He heard a sea gull scream and opened his eyes to find the sky empty and the beach deserted. Inge, sensing he wanted to be alone, had begun to walk along the shore, looking for sea shells. Far beyond her, a boy and a girl walked holding hands. Before him, a dog went sniffing to the water's edge then ran back from a breaking wave. Immobile on a nearby log, a lizard nourished itself with the sun—as he was doing. And across the dry, empty strand there came the salt smell of wave foam, bringing with it an acute and almost painful sense of spring. Without forethought, he spoke then to Pope John, in a familiar fashion, as though he were sitting nearby.

"I think even you, Giovanni, would like this because within yourself you also feel these true and solemn searchings."

The sound of his voice disturbed him. So he remained silent for a while, and felt better. Nature was to be taken that way—to be loved but not questioned. Her secrets were not revealed upon demand, since revelation came as a gift and not a reply. Within the silence, the waves like tumbling green bells brought a murmuring of voices across the empty beach. Then suddenly, across a broader stretch of time, the poet Montale's words came back with the inrushing tide:

> *Ancient one, I am drunk with the voice*
> *That escapes from your mouths when they lift clear*
> *Like green bells and throw themselves back*
> *And break up . . .*

116

An Artist and the Pope

. . . you were the first to tell me
That the tiny seething
Of my heart was nothing more than a moment
Of yours; that in my depths
Was your perilous law: to be vast and diverse
And yet to be bound:
And so to clear myself of every filthiness
As do you who dash upon the shores
Among the cork bits, seaweed, starfishes,
The fruitless rubbish of your void.

—Those old laws of the sea engulfed the world, including you and me, Giovanni. For did you not tell me that you felt your heart to be vast and manifold—yet contained—within its love for God? And did you not call your bishops from around the world to sit in a great Vatican Council in order to throw out fruitless rubbish from your void?

—You did this, as you explained it, to tighten the links between man and God. Just so, I seek to tighten the link between myself and those few works or sculptures of which I am capable, throwing out all that separates me from the primary source of energy which is rooted in human life. A painting or a sculpture is a gesture of love toward others. And within that gesture, I gave my promise to finish the doors, Giovanni, to you as a human being and not as a Pope. Yet how can I now keep that promise and still hold on to the roots of my powers?

Lying on the beach, Manzù tried to think it out in simple terms: If he took Mary and Christ down from heaven, and began them again on their earthly trip, how far could he go with them? The answer was simple: to the moment of death.

—And if we stopped there, what would we have?

—We would have Christ the man, believed by many

to be the Son of God, killed by violence. And in Mary we would see the beauty of grace and love. Hail Mary, full of Grace.

—Hail yourself. Does that say everything?

—It says more than showing two figures floating in heaven with weightless angels. It says that two people are dying and in such a moment you do not look at death but at life which is leaving—that final uncoupling of mind and body which makes man both spiritual and human. So here the meaning of Christ and Mary is most evident. For in their manner of dying, one can understand how they lived and so deserved a heaven—if there ever happens to be one.

—But that is not important?

—Life is important. And its godlike gift is most evident at the moment it is being taken from man by violence or cruelty or greed or any of the other natural disasters which could be shown on the other panels of the door.

—So why not do that and make them all dead or dying?

Excitedly, he sat upright asking himself: Why not? Why not the Doors of Death? Ghiberti had made the Doors of Paradise for the Baptistry in Florence and Rodin had cast his Gate of Hell. His could show the beauty of life and at the same time it could be a great shout, a violent protest in bronze against cruelty and violence and all else which steals life from man.

He jumped up and hastened down the beach toward Inge. She must have known from his walk that he had solved the problem, for she began to run toward him. They met at the water's edge, saying each other's name over and over as though they both had survived a terrible danger.

Some sea shells fell from her pocket onto the wet sand, and they quickly bent to pick them up before the waves took them away. One of them was especially beautiful, its purple interior flecked with gold as rich as the cape of a Renaissance prince.

Where, he wondered, was this bright mollusk when it slipped across the line? How far was it below the sea and beyond the reach of the unsleeping tide which finally seized it, fruitless rubbish at last, to cast it upon the shore? What final error caused this?

Sometimes one awaits
To discover an error in Nature
The dead point of the world, the link that does not hold,
The thread to disentangle, which finally places us
In the middle of a truth.

Yes, these doors of death would hang on the last thread of life and so disentangle it, little by little, to drop us finally like exhausted lovers into the middle of a truth —wherever it was.

"Do you think don Giuseppe will approve?"

"Of course he will," said Inge. "He's the only one involved who knows anything about art—and you."

"If he doesn't, then I can't continue. Because he must arrange for the commission to accept it. Only he can do that."

"He will."

"If he doesn't, I will have to go to Pope John and say that I can do the doors only in this way."

"I say he will."

"Don't be too sure. It's a big change."

They were in the car, on the way back to town. He had tried phoning don Giuseppe, but was unable to find him. Earlier, the priest had called Manzù's house, leaving two numbers—his publishing house and a doctor's office.

But he had already left both places. Now it was twilight and, as they approached Rome, the traffic became heavy and slow which only increased Manzù's anxiety to get home.

"He's trying to reach me, too."

"He knew you were worried."

"Maybe the Pope told him something else, after I left."

"Does the Pope know the terrible way these doors have been handled?"

"I don't know. Perhaps don Giuseppe told him."

"He should know," said Inge. "Somebody should tell him about it."

"It's been in the newspapers."

"No," she said. "Not all of it."

Inge was right. The story of the doors had not been told, especially its strange beginning. This happened during the reign of Pius XII, with the death of a canon of St. Peter's who had been a rich Bavarian nobleman before becoming a priest late in life. In his will, the former Prince Georg von Bayern left his fortune to be spent on new bronze doors for St. Peter's. Depending upon how much the doors would cost, the former prince proposed replacing one, two, or even all of three wooden doors standing on either side of a fifteenth-century bronze door by Filarete. If the Vatican agreed to do this, the dead Bavarian expected to be happy in the hereafter. Otherwise, his money was to go to a German naval academy in Bremen where he had also spent many happy years before joining the forces of the Lord.

This was in May, 1943, when it seemed that the German navy did not need much help. It had just had a very busy year sinking Allied ships. The tide of World War II had not yet fully turned against it and some people even imagined that such a mighty navy would last longer on this earth than St. Peter's.

But a choice had to be made: either doors for the Pope's basilica, or cadets for Hitler's warships. The Vatican had five years to choose an artist for the doors and ten years to put up at least one of them. Faced with this problem of choice and the conflict in Europe, it did what it normally does in such difficult moments: nothing.

Finally, one day early in 1947, Pope Pius was reminded that he had to order up the doors, or give up the money. By this time, however, there was no longer a German navy, so it was not clear just how the money could be given away —unless it was split between the Americans and Russians then occupying Germany who could in turn hand it over to their own navies. This was never seriously examined, however, since Papa Pacelli had no intention of allowing the money to go north.

The basic problem was to find a sculptor to do the work. In previous centuries, this was a much easier task. Someone like Julius II could commission a Michelangelo to work on his back in the Sistine Chapel, Raphael on his knees in the loggia, and Bramante on a scaffolding in the wings. But as Pope John observed, the artists had all moved out. For this reason, the prince's will stipulated that a commission be created to select the sculptor by international competition.

Normally such a commission should know something about art and architecture. But the Commission for the Bronze Doors of the Most Holy Basilica of Saint Peter in the Vatican knew little about the fine arts, having specialized more in theology, canon law and the art of survival in the Roman Curia. They were therefore in the position of someone who is color blind on a butterfly hunt and never sure of just what he has in the net.

At the first international competition, between July and December, for example, they collected eighty-four entries for two separate twin-leaf doors. They then proceeded to peer at these works, much as a puzzled motorist looks under the hood of his automobile. Finally, with some outside help, in March, 1948, they picked twelve of the biggest names and asked the competing sculptors to submit more developed studies for a final selection.

Manzù had entered the competition with the intention of dedicating the doors to his mother. She had been a pious soul, and this was an honor he wanted to give her. It was also a great challenge to create the first doors in 500 years for St. Peter's. With this in mind, he never thought the commission's theme for the doors would eventually become an iconographic nightmare. At that time, he had not begun to break away from the Church. His series on "Christ in Our Humanity" had brought attacks in 1941 from the Fascists, the Vatican newspaper, *L'Osservatore Romano*, and the Catholic press. But that had happened during the war, and the other shocks were yet to come.

But by the time they got around to judging the work of the twelve finalists, in the fall of 1949, the Christ series had been shown in Rome, the Holy Office had censored Manzù and he had suffered his sad encounter with Pius XII. Deep inside, some doubts were growing. He had not given up his belief, however, nor did he intend to give up the doors.

His feelings became even further entrenched after he was blocked by monsignori within the Curia who favored other sculptors, and had insinuated that Manzù was dangerous. A whispering campaign was launched describing him as a communist and a freemason unfit to do doors. His lack of Christian faith, they said, was evident in his work.

Cardinal Costantini cited as example of this one of Manzù's proposed panels showing the death of St. Gregory VII. It portrayed the seated saint as being held upright, while

PAVLVS·V·PONT·MAX·ANNO·XIIII

The Doors of Death
St. Peter's

Death of Mary

(FROM THE PRIVATE
COLLECTION OF
GIACOMO MANZÙ)

Death of Christ

Eucharistic symbol: Vine branch

Eucharistic symbol: Sheaves of wheat

Relief group, lower left portal

Death of Abel

Death of St. Joseph

Death by Violence

Death of John XXIII

Detail, Death of John XXIII

Relief group, lower right portal

Death of St. Stephen

Death of Gregory VII

Death in Space

Death on Earth

Detail, Death on Earth

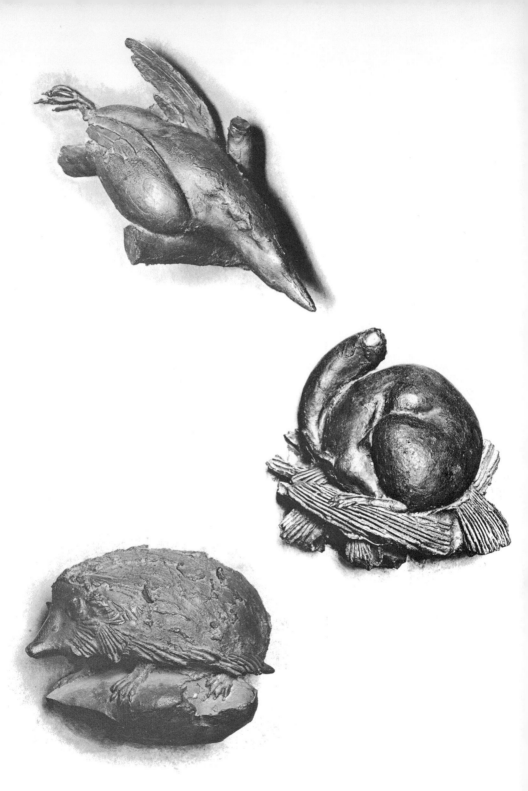

Dove, Dormouse, Hedgehog
Base of left portal

Owl, Turtle and Snake, Raven
Base of right portal

Opening of the Second Vatican Council
Frieze on reverse right portal of door

(FROM THE PRIVATE COLLECTION OF GIACOMO MANZÙ)

(FROM THE PRIVATE COLLECTION OF GIACOMO MANZÙ)

Opening of the Second Vatican Council
Frieze on reverse left portal

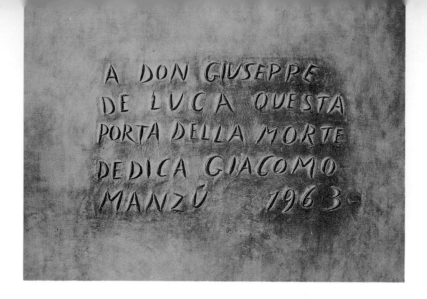

Dedication of the Doors

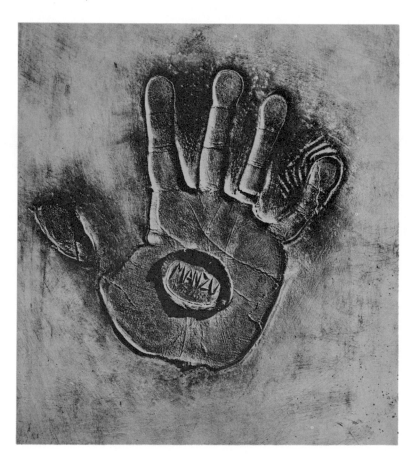

Signature of Giacomo Manzù

Portrait bust of Pope John XXIII, 1963, bronze
Vatican Library Collection

Manzù at work on death mask
of Pope John XXIII, 1967

Medal, 1960
Olympic Games

Medal, 1962
Vatican Council

Medal, 1964
First Anniversary of Death of Pope John XXIII

Manzù at work on bust of Inge, 1967

Ballerina, 1962

(FROM THE PRIVATE COLLECTION OF GIACOMO MANZÙ)

Pope John XXIII sitting for head by Manzù

Pope John XXIII and Giacomo Manzù
Autographed by the Pope

the papal crown rested at his feet. The cardinal pointed to this to prove that Manzu had no respect for the papacy. Otherwise why would he put so sacred a symbol of the papacy upon the ground? Someone recalled that Raphael had done the same thing, but this did not deter the cardinal from sustaining that Popes should die with their tiaras on. About this time, several members of the commission let it be known they would advise the Pope to return the money to the Germans, or even give it to the devil himself, rather than award the doors to the Bergamasque freemason and Moscow agent, Giacomo Manzu.

When it appeared that the award would go to other sculptors, a campaign to defend Manzù began in the Italian press and quickly grew into massive proportions. One after another, major Italian papers criticized the commission and the Vatican for failing to comprehend serious art. Some of them, such as Turin's *La Nuova Stampa*, used rather strong language:

"The best work is that of Giacomo Manzù. His saints and popes and cardinals are all solid creatures. But they have already been condemned to hell . . . the Bergamasque sculptor has been accused of masonry and communism which is sheer calumny. The Vatican has long ceased to be the great art patron of the golden centuries. Today it satisfies itself with stamps, cheap tapestries and funereal monuments."

Milan's *Corriere della Sera* used even heavier artillery:

"As in the first show, the best work, by a long shot, is that of Giacomo Manzu. But the commission can't make up its mind. The Church should always favor real artists when they show their willingness to work with religious art. But unfortunately it helps false artists. We've now reached the limit with some people falsely accusing Manzù of communism and masonry, when anybody knows he is a faithful

Catholic. At any rate, if the Church had to trust only the purest saints, San Luca and Beato Angelico alone would have worked for it over the centuries."

As could be expected, such attacks soon aroused Pope Pius, who ordered the commission to do their job in a way which did not cause the Holy See to look ridiculous. Facing such pressures, the conspiracy within the commission began to crumble. They made a last-minute rally by seeking outside advice from other government and cultural bodies, but when none of these would submit to sharing public responsibility for a decision beyond their private control, the commission had nowhere to hide its maneuvers and so was forced to recognize the work of the man from Bergamo.

They awarded the work on the three doors to three different artists, giving Manzù the extreme left one. He received his commission last, but soon was far ahead of the others. His work was to be the first to go up, setting the pace for those that were to follow.

"You should ask Monsignor de Luca if he has told Pope John how much you suffered to do these doors."

"He knows it."

"Monsignor de Luca does not know all the answers."

"What do you mean, Inge?"

"Like this change you are making. It comes from your heart and it has no answer in books. I know the monsignor is a very learned man, but if he doesn't see the answer in a book, he might say no."

"He won't."

"If he does, you must say you are right. Don't let him impose his formulas on you."

"All right, all right."

As soon as they arrived at the apartment, he called Monsignor de Luca again and this time found him at home.

124

Normally the priest went to bed early to read. So he asked him:

"Are you already in bed?"

"Not yet—why?"

"I need to see you because I have something urgent about the work."

"The portrait or the doors?"

"The doors."

There was muffling on the line. It was not clear whether don Giuseppe was swallowing some food, or sitting down with the phone.

"You made the Pope happy by promising to do them, Giacomo."

"I'm glad."

"You haven't changed your mind, have you?"

"No, but I have a new solution which I want to explain to you. I have decided to make them all dead—Christ, Mary, the saints, all of them. But not as much dead as dying, because it will be a way of looking back into their lives . . ."

He stopped, feeling terribly frustrated. For thirteen years he had been wrestling with this great ghost in his heart and in his home. Now it hung in a balance and he was trying to save it over a telephone. *Porca miseria.* As usual, don Giuseppe sensed his discomfort.

"Come over, Giacomo. Come over now."

When he got there, the monsignor had his collar off, and there was a bottle of cold Marino wine on the table. Manzù recounted his drive to the beach and how he found the solution for the doors. Don Giuseppe liked it, but foresaw trouble.

"You will have some opposition. On the other hand, the doors assigned to you are often called the Doors of Death. So it is logical, and we can approach it that way."

This was true and Manzù had forgotten it. Or perhaps

he had unconsciously come to terms with it. Through these doors the bodies of dead cardinals and prelates were brought into the basilica. At any rate, it was now important that this title not focus the concept of the doors onto death alone.

"These are not doors looking at death. They are in support of life against what causes death, against the ways in which a man's life is stolen from him by cruelty, by violence, by natural disaster and all those things which happen to man—so that, seeing this, we sense that life has beauty and dignity and worth and he who steals it is not only a criminal against the victim, but against all society, against you and me and everybody."

De Luca nodded that he agreed and refilled their wine glasses.

"So you can have St. Stephen crushed by stones as the first Christian martyr," he said. "Also Cain killing Abel in man's first death, and a violent one, too."

"All right, but we can also have people of today. Because the martyrs of our time are not just your legendary saints. They are ordinary men and women, anonymous people in everyday life, who suffer and die in obscurity. These, too, must be on the doors."

"Sure, sure," he said, obviously still thinking of his Church saints and how they would look on the doors.

"Sure, sure," he said again. "So now you can make Christ with Eve and the Madonna with Adam."

"Christ with whom?"

"At the foot of the Cross, you can put Eve. And at the foot of the expired Madonna, you put Adam."

"I'll think about it."

They were silent for a moment, then Manzù said: "You are causing some confusion, because you are limiting me to two figures. What if I need three of them?"

"*Beh* . . . you'll just have to make do!"

Manzù laughed with him, but it was not all that funny. The moment had come to make sure they understood one another.

"I might need three people, my dear *monsignore*, because the answer to this is not in a book and we can't impose any prefixed formulas or saints upon it. It has to come from my hands as I do it."

"All right, but it has to also come from your friend, the Pope."

"Why?"

"Because you can only do this if he agrees to it. Once he accepts it, the commission will more likely fall in line."

"So you will tell him?"

"No, Giacomo. It's better you explain it yourself. At your next meeting."

Manzù agreed to this, but not without some fear that he might fail completely. It had not been easy with don Giuseppe, who knew him quite well. So it would be even more difficult with the Pope.

Chapter Eleven

MANZÙ'S meeting with Pope
John came a few days after his visit with Monsignor de
Luca. As instructed, he explained the new concept for
the doors and the Pope seemed to grasp it immediately.

"You intend to show everyone, including the Madonna
and our Savior, in their human aspect?"

"Sì, Santità."

For a moment John said nothing more. Manzù was
in the midst of sketching him and there was only the sound
of charcoal on paper. They were in the papal library, with
John seated in the golden chair by the window, while Monsignor de Luca stood nearby. It was the fifth encounter, on
a May afternoon, and Manzù had begun the session doing
sketches—feeling it was easier to talk while drawing, rather
than working in clay. Also, he wanted some linear studies for
reference in his studio when doing final work on the busts.

When John finally spoke, it was evident he had been
thinking about the proposal to portray Christ and the Madonna on earth and not in heaven.

"It doesn't mean they are any the less for it," he said.
"In fact, it could show the reality of their presence in our
lives today and how they exist with us everywhere—in

129

our homes, in the streets, and wherever we are. That reality must always be made evident, though it should not be overlooked that the Resurrection is the greatest victory of Christ. For it is the mystery of death challenged and defeated and an assurance of victory for the Holy Roman Church."

As far as Manzù could make out, this indicated John would approve of the two top panels. There remained the smaller ones below, and the Pope spoke next of these.

"As for the saints and martyrs," he said, "you will show them dying with their faith. And the others, the men and women you mention, if they are seen in their dignity as human beings, with their capacity for belief and love, you will have revealed the visible basis for the living Church."

He looked at Monsignor de Luca who nodded agreement. With that, Manzù's heart began to pound excitedly and he nodded mute thanks and gratitude to them both. Finally, he had the consent to undertake the great challenge before him!

"All that remains," added the Pope, "is for the commission to approve it."

What did that mean? Manzù glanced at don Giuseppe, who made a sign to drop the matter. The sculptor agreed and, putting aside his drawing pad, began to work on the second clay bust. About that time the door opened and Monsignor Capovilla brought in Manzù's son, Pio, to introduce him to the Pope. The Pope's secretary never failed to display infinite courtesy and understanding, and as the sculptor's love for Pope John grew, so did his respect and affection for don Loris Capovilla.

After that interruption, work on the clay portrait went ahead without any more loss of time and by the end of the session it had been brought to the point where it could be finished in the studio. Yet even this head did not satisfy

Manzù and he wanted to start another one. Pope John understood it without being told.

"You will come again soon?"

"Sì, *Santità*, although I am ashamed to take so much of your time."

"Don't worry about that. There is always a free moment and it is a pleasure to meet with you. Also, we have many things to look at together."

Capovilla showed them out. On the way, Manzù again expressed his discomfort at taking so much of the Pope's time.

"The Holy Father enjoys your company," he replied, "and is willing to continue until you are satisfied with your work. Also, he enjoys talking with the monsignor."

"How much one learns from every meeting!" exclaimed don Giuseppe. "His humanity is what Ariosto would call 'good taste in poetry'—a secret gift. At the same time, he's a man like a mountain and that's Giacomo's great challenge. How can he manage to pull it all down into one lump of clay small enough to hold between your two hands?"

"How well you see it," agreed Capovilla with a deep sigh and a shake of the head, indicating he knew better than anyone else the immensity of the mountain where he labored and lived.

They entered the Sala Clementina. A picket of Swiss Guards sprang to attention. Then as they walked through the vast, silent hall, there was the thud of oaken halberd staffs striking the floor, the shuffling of feet and a curious squeaking of Capovilla's shoes which sounded like a parrot being throttled. They emerged finally onto the glassed-in loggia above San Damaso courtyard and, looking out toward St. Peter's, began to talk about the new concept for the doors.

Manzù was worried about the Pope's saying it would be necessary to clear it with the commission. He had hoped John's approval would be final.

"Do you think it can be blocked by the commission?" he asked.

"We will talk to them," said Capovilla.

"If the Pope likes the idea, how can they possibly go against him?"

"You know how things are done here," said Capovilla. "It takes time and the right way of going about it."

"I hope I made it clear that I can't go ahead with it the way they want it and that this is the only solution possible for me."

"Yes," said Capovilla.

An usher in red brocade knee breeches and buckled shoes came in haste to say that Monsignor Capovilla was wanted in the Pope's library. The sculptor and the priest said goodbye. Manzù watched him leave—a lean, intense young man with the crew haircut of an astronaut, the creaking shoes of a country priest, and a black cassock flapping about his ankles as he hurried back to the Pope who was as big as a mountain. He thought again of Capovilla's sensitivity and what enormous sacrifices were required of one living perpetually in the shadow of such a man.

"It must be like serving Mass around the clock, with no Saturdays off," said Manzù, as they turned to go down to San Damaso.

"It's worse," said don Giuseppe. "The Pope's secretary shares the Pontiff's burden, but none of the glory. First, he is privy to many of the great papal secrets and as a result is cut off from all other men. Next, if the Pope is a prisoner of the Vatican, he is a prisoner of a prisoner. Further, if the Pope has enemies—as they all do, including Pope John— they are also enemies of the secretary. Finally, when the

132

Pope dies, he leaves his younger secretary powerless, at last, before the waiting field of enemies who quickly assemble around the new pontiff."

"Then what happens?"

"It's an unwritten rule that each Pope protects the secretary of his predecessor by giving him some job within the pontifical household. If they are adroit, they go up in the ranks—like Confalonieri, who was secretary to Pius IX, and now is a cardinal."

"Which can happen to Capovilla, because he is very bright and dedicated."

Don Giuseppe shook his head.

"Yes, but those two qualities can be a liability. In the Curia you are expected to be loyal, yet benign—like a polyp, not a man. Capovilla is a man and he loves his Holy Father with a fierce loyalty which has set people against him. Some even claim he oversteps his role as secretary."

"Does he?"

"When two such selfless men live and work together, a certain fusion of ideas, if not of roles, is inevitable. A private secretary to a Pope—especially a modern one whose role can be more complicated than many heads of state—must become an executive arm. He works closely with the Holy Father, helping with his thoughts and projects, just as he helps him serve Mass each morning, adjust the television, or assist him in and out of an automobile."

"What's wrong with that?"

"Nothing, until a cardinal or a powerful monsignor from a congregation gets John to change a decision. Capovilla, learning about it, might remind John of his original thinking and so cause him to change it back. Or someone else might do it. Or the Pope might do it himself. However it happens, the cardinal or monsignor thinks it was Capovilla. So they chalk up one more reason to get his scalp as soon as it can be done safely—that is when the Pope is dead and the secretary, bound by secrecy, cannot publicly fight his enemies."

"And my doors," said Manzù, "will probably increase his crop of enemies."

"Yes, because the commission wants no interference, from the Pope or his secretary."

"How will they oppose it?"

"In the way it's done in the Roman Curia—through the back door."

"The Pope's?"

"Yes."

"When can we expect it?"

"When you least expect it. When you think you have beaten the Curia conservatives, they come back out of the wallpaper and the filing cases. It's incredible. But they can't reach you, Giacomo, as long as Pope John is with you. When will you start work?"

"As soon as I do one more model of John. Maybe after the next sitting if there aren't too many interruptions."

But there were interruptions at their next encounter, some delightful, others surprising—beginning with Pope John, who greeted Manzù most warmly as he came trundling into the library with a portfolio of sketches and fresh clay to begin the third bust.

"Sculptor," he said, "you are a book where one is perpetually surprised to find oneself still at the beginning."

Manzù reacted, for a moment, as he would have in the rough world outside—taking this as a veiled joke at his continual inability to finish the portrait. Then he stopped, knowing that such play on the ineptitude of someone else was not John's way. And looking at him, he found eyes searching into his which said he was right.

"The world turns with those who look at the stars,

and I'm touched, *Santità*, that you should look at me."

"Ah!" he said, happily, "my feeling comes from looking both at you and your work. What have you brought us today?"

Manzù quickly opened the portfolio of various sketches he had made in ink, tempera and watercolor—studies of the strong and human face that he had yet to model to his complete satisfaction. Had he brought them to justify himself before the Pope? Maybe. Manzù did not know, but was pleased to see that John liked them. He liked them so much that after looking at them once, John drew a pair of spectacles from his cassock and did it all over again.

"Let's keep them all together," he said, "because when the bust is completed this can be a documentation of the work and presented with the finished bronze."

"The Vatican is a big place," said Manzù, "they might get lost here."

"Lost?" said the Pope. "Why would they get lost if we knew where they were?"

The sculptor did not want to contradict him, and said nothing. There had been pressure on him to publish the drawings in a commercial venture which had nothing to do with their worth or with the dignity of the Pope. Regardless, these were sketches of a work in progress, not finished drawings. So with the exception of two or three, he intended to destroy them all.

"Nothing's lost in the Vatican," said Pope John, "because everything's tied down—including the Pope himself. In fact, you can hardly move anything around here."

They all laughed and don Giuseppe graciously noted: "Not quite, *Santità*, if you call a Vatican Council to update the Church and hold three consistories to create forty-one new cardinals."

Manzù had already set up his stand and begun to work

135

on a new clay form—the third portrait. Everything seemed perfect. From the window, an unusually warm light fell upon John, who seemed relaxed and naturally himself. With this possibility before him, the artist quickly fell into the rhythm of his work. Yet before he had gone very far, John raised a question.

"Have you met the cardinal from Bukoba?"

"Who?"

"Cardinal Rugambwa."

"No, *Santità*."

"A most intelligent man, with a rare faith."

He repeated the word "rare" again, saying it softly and almost to himself—as if to emphasize that this was a faith which rode above that of most other men.

"When Rugambwa was made cardinal, he became ill. Even more, the news so disturbed him that he suffered a minor heart attack. He is one *Signor Cardinale* you should know. You would like him very much. For he is a true man and full of faith."

Manzù replied he would be pleased to meet such a *Signor Cardinale* and John promised to arrange it. Don Giuseppe then said he understood how Rugambwa could suffer a heart attack.

"If you tell a deeply religious man that he is to be a cardinal, it can be a real shock," he said. "But here we also have a man who, born in a mud hut, barely one generation away from the tribal drum beat, suddenly becomes the first of his race in all history to be a prince of the Roman Church. The pressures on him to be the perfect prototype—without error and thus not human—must be so fierce that only a saint could withstand it."

"Yes, yes," said the Pope.

Then he smiled and said: "You know, when he was made cardinal, not everyone was in agreement. But I thought—

beh! let's do it, let's make him cardinal. A little bit of black in so much white will give us a nice *caffè-latte.*"

As they laughed at this, Manzù thought he saw something unique about John. He had his enemies, but he refused to identify them as such. In making the Negro a cardinal, he found that "not everyone was in agreement." This did not mean, however, that there was permanent opposition against him or the Negro. At the most, it was temporary, since faith or truth would sooner or later bring everyone together. The opposition was no more permanent or personal than a nightfall, or a leak in a rooftop.

"So finish the doors for St. Peter's," said John, "but don't take on anything else since you can never tell what the Lord will put into our heads. It could be that you might have to build a cathedral in Tanganyika."

"All right," replied Manzù. "If I am asked to do it by you, I will be architect, sculptor and painter. But if it's for anyone else, no."

The Pope said no more, nor did the sculptor. Their conversations often began and ended that way, without continuing links. But the suddenness of such an offer and his own unexpected reply left Manzù dazed.

He turned back to working the clay, asking himself: What in the devil are you doing? You decided long ago to do no more work for the Church. Then you agree to do this bust, then the doors, and now you talk about doing a cathedral from top to bottom, including mosaics, painting, sculpture—the works. Are you going to stop this stuff or not?

He tried to put it out of his mind, but it would not go and the form of the cathedral began to take shape. He saw it as great shell, open to the sky. The walls would be several yards high, but without a fixed roof, so that those sitting in church could view birds in flight or the night's slow-moving stars. The art would relate to the land and the people and show the new cities, the villages, the rivers, the jungles, the banana trees. Or did they have banana trees in Tanganyika?

Pope John had begun to retell the story of Manzù's father tugging at his hem. It was more or less the same as before, except this time Manzù's father had even more enthusiasm for the sermon, saying: *"Forza*, don Angelo! Keep going, you're doing great!" John's added enjoyment indicated that since he and the sculptor knew each other better now, they could better appreciate the evidence that they belonged together on a pulpit stairway, if not in the same family pew.

With that over, Manzù concentrated on his work, while John and don Giuseppe discussed subjects dear to them. There were no further interruptions and all went well until Monsignor Capovilla came into the library.

"Santità, it is necessary that you appear for a benediction."

"Ah sì? Is there some pilgrimage?"

"No, no. There are some soldiers."

"Some soldiers?"

"About two hundred American soldiers."

"Ah so? Then I'd better go."

He got out of his chair, adjusted his *zucchetto* and prepared to leave. But before going, he put his hand on Manzù's shoulder and said: "Listen, sculptor. Let's do something. You wait here, and I'll finish quickly. I'll bless them and come back, so we can have another half hour together."

"Thank you, *Santità*. That's fine with me."

Manzù wanted the extra time, hoping it would allow him to finish the bust. So he waited, working on the base of the portrait, while don Giuseppe sat nearby writing some notes—until Monsignor Capovilla returned in his usual hurried manner, without the Pope.

"You might as well go," he said. "He's still in there and

there are several hundred American soldiers around him, listening to his stories. I could have told you he would not come back immediately, because it's impossible for him to bless people and then turn away. That's why he hates doing it from a window or a balcony. He likes to get right in there with them and feel for himself that there's no wall between them."

Manzù resignedly suggested they could finish the portrait at another sitting. Capovilla agreed and said good-bye, hastily scooping papers from the Pope's desk as he hurried out. Manzù and don Giuseppe followed. On the way out, they heard loud clapping from the Sala Concistoro.

"No wall there," said Manzù.

The clapping became more intense, with cheers and whistles, followed by some hip-hip-hoorays.

"Not only no wall in there," said don Giuseppe. "It sounds like all the others in the Apostolic Palace are tumbling down."

After their next encounter two weeks later, Manzù considered the work sufficiently complete to finish it in the studio. Before he left, John asked if he would consent to do some medallions for the Olympic Games, to be held in Rome in August. It was already mid-June, which meant the work had to be done rather rapidly. Despite this and the pressure of other work, Manzù agreed to do it.

"All right," he said. "It will be an honor to do a medal for the athletes of all nations, which is to be given to them by you."

"There is not much time in which to do it," said don Giuseppe.

"It doesn't matter," said Pope John. "He can do it so fast that it will be the first record of the Olympic Games!"

On parting, John did not say *addio*, meaning "good-

139

bye"—but rather *arrivederci*, meaning "until we see each other again." And he said it with his arm about the sculptor, leaving the sensation that they would know each other forever—or until the moment of death.

A few days later, Monsignor Capovilla came to the studio to say that the commission for St. Peter's doors appeared willing to accept the proposed changes. This was great news and Manzù thanked him warmly for his help and understanding. Now he was free to begin the great labor which lay before him like an unscaled mountain.

Capovilla explained further that Pope John wanted Manzù to have a completely free hand.

"He spoke to Cardinal Testa about you. He told him to look after you."

"He what?"

"He said to him—'*Beh*, I spoke to Manzù about the doors. If you want to stay near him, he will be doing the Doors of Death. If you stand by him, I will be in agreement.'"

"To stay near me—what does that mean? How near?"

"In the event you need help, you can call him."

"But if I don't need help, he does not have to stand near me?"

Capovilla nodded that was how he understood it and Manzù was satisfied. There was only the great mountain before him. All he had to do was scale it—alone. At least that was what he thought. For the final battle of the doors had not yet begun.

Chapter Twelve

T<small>HE</small> next weeks and months tumbled one upon the other in rapid succession, as Manzù sought to meet the greatest challenge of his life—to place upon the doors of St. Peter's as much as he could of the grace and beauty of human life, of its precious worth, and the shameful crime of violence which took it away. And once started, he became even more excited by it. Here was something worth saying in our time. Here he would be able to pour out everything he felt and knew up to that moment in his life.

Trouble lay ahead, however, within the substance of the work itself. Manzù's concept was to create figures from the world of the living, men and women capable of uttering curses and cries of anguish as they went into their death— an event which Christianity teaches should be met by resignation, prayer, and faith. So the doors were destined to find their opponents, and their creation eventually became a battle fought on two fronts: Manzù struggling to realize his dream inside the studio, while outside cardinals and monsignori of the commission sought to control and even alter it.

This scandalous and illegal invasion of the artist's studio grew as the enemy had an objective to attack—that is, when the figures began to emerge on the doors. Until that happened, the main struggle was within Manzù, to release from himself the men and women, the saints and sinners who were to people a bronze world 25 feet high, 11 feet wide and 8 inches deep.

Yet before he could do that, it was necessary to divide up the world in which they were to live—to break down the vast surface into inhabitable sections or panels. He had already done this in earlier studies and now, on the final assault, he found still further variations were needed. A key area was the base, below the bottom panels, which had been 23½, then 27½ inches. When it was enlarged to 31½, everything above it worked. Finally there was a harmony between the separate panels which would continue to hold together as a total unity when each one was invested with the people who were to inhabit their depths.

The "depth" of each panel was, of course, another challenge in the scaling of the doors. This had to be in harmony with the surface. For the doors were not a screen or a flat diaphragm separating a church interior from the outside world, but rather a three-dimensional work which had its own projection in depth toward a distant horizon.

Yet how far away should the horizon be? How deep the perspective before the earth and sky and water ran together? This was basic, for it affected the handling of every panel. In Ghiberti's Doors of Paradise, for example, each panel is a separate happening, as on a stage where the actors play their roles before a background optically designed to suggest greater space than the stage itself. But there remains always an end—a point where the eye, seeking the final point in depth, comes to its spawning finish. In doing this, it races beyond the principal figures, by-passing the immediate drama for an adventure of its own. It takes a side trip, not intended by the artist.

Manzù intended to eliminate such distracting trips by removing all perspective and leaving the players on a limitless horizon. Beyond them, the earth and sky and water never meet—or they have already met, so that the observer finds himself in the total unity of man and matter. In doing this, Manzù would reverse Ghiberti's perspective—or stand on the far side of it, beyond the point where all lines meet, allowing one to look back toward the beginning.

With this in mind, he chose to work in low relief, bringing the background out, rather than in—as he had done in the panels of Christ in our Humanity, and as he had done with the doors for the Salzburg Cathedral. Yet when it was all ready, he had trouble beginning and not even don Giuseppe could help.

"When are you going to the top?" asked the priest, one day in October.

"To where?"

"Up to the top, to do the big ones."

"*Beh*, when I've got it figured out."

"What's blocking you?"

"Mary. I see Christ, but I don't have her figured out yet."

They were in the studio, waiting for a visit of Monsignor Capovilla with some members of the commission. Before them was a full scale model in plaster of the doors. It went up 25 feet and from below seemed immense. The panels were marked off, ready for their figures, but this did not reduce the enormity of the great white façade. On one side, a 30 foot ladder ran to the top panels where Christ and Mary were to be shown in their moment of death.

For months Manzù had been like a man going around the base of a mountain he wished to climb, making all the preparations with occasional glimpses at the snow white peak above him. He had created two crossed sheaves of wheat and the entwined grape stems to go on the doors in place of ring handles. These were symbols of man's food on earth and, for all who believed, the Eucharistic link between

145

Christ above and man below. He had also created twenty-four birds and animals, obtaining from these six which he liked and would put along the bottom of the door. Both of these themes had been used successfully on his doors for the Salzburg Cathedral which otherwise suffered in being limited to four saints with whom he had little identity. And lastly, he had begun a long strip to go on the reverse side of the doors, showing a procession of bishops entering the Vatican Council with Cardinal Rugambwa kneeling before Pope John, who loved him in a special way.

These he had done by putting everything else aside, even the busts of the Pope, and now the time had come to go up onto the doors and place there the men and women, living and dying, who still remained somewhere within him. Yet blocking it all was Mary—or, rather, his inability to determine how he could represent her.

"You have the Madonna and Christ," said don Giuseppe, looking up at the two top empty panels.

"That's right and they don't balance."

"Why not? Each has his panel. On the right, Christ will be seen on the Cross, while on the left the Madonna is dying—or falling asleep before her assumption into heaven."

"It doesn't work. There's not enough weight in Mary to balance off the drama of the Cross. Iconographically, the crucifixion of Christ outweighs the dormition of the Virgin."

They were silent for a moment, staring up at the white face of plaster.

"Even if I make her an adolescent Madonna—as in Michelangelo's *Pietà*—a dying beauty can't equal the murder of a man like Christ."

"Look, Giacomo, you can put on anybody you like. There's no record of where or how Mary died. Or who was with her when it happened. Caravaggio surrounds her with a bunch of disciples."

"Who are a lot of weeping old men with beards. That's not the weight I need.

"Well, if you put Eve at the foot of the Cross, you can put Adam at the foot of the Virgin."

"What the hell does Adam have to do with the Virgin?"

"I don't know, Giacomo. Your trouble is that you exclude the greatest drama of the Virgin's death—her bodily assumption into heaven."

"That's not the answer," he said. "At least, not for me because I want to tell the human drama, not the mystical one."

"What is the answer then?"

"I don't know. *Porca miseria,* I just don't know, except that something is wrong here. It doesn't work."

They began to look through some rough sketches Manzù had made of the dying Virgin, surrounded by men and women witnessing the tragic moment. These remained, for him, little more than tight and meaningless clusters of people. Their shock and sorrow did not add to the Virgin's grace or beauty. And since no testimonial was needed for her living, their presence at the moment of death was an invasion of privacy. It robbed death of its dignity.

"I have to get rid of these people."

"Maybe you need some symbolic angels," said don Giuseppe.

"To do what?"

"To witness the event."

"The witnesses should be the people looking at it on the doors, no one else."

"Angels," persisted don Giuseppe, "to carry her into heaven."

"I'm sorry, but that doesn't convince me."

Monsignor Capovilla entered with some members of the commission. There were five of them and after allowing them to stare at the towering white façade of the doors,

Manzù began to show some of the work already done—the grain and grape stalks, and the animals. He was especially fond of an owl which looked very wise and sober. In Greek culture it stood for wisdom, but sometimes in Christianity it also represented death. He thought this would please the visitors, and it did. He also liked the tortoise snapping off the snake's head. It was a struggle which intrigued him and they seemed to like it, too.

Before he could go much further, one of the monsignori went up to the doors and indicated the base with the toe of his black shoe.

"If you narrowed this space," he said, "you could make all the panels above it bigger and have room for more."

"What?"

"Drop these bottom panels lower and you will have more space up above," he said again.

It was so incredible that Manzù could hardly believe it even the second time. He looked at Capovilla who saw the Bergamasque's face going black and quickly sought to stop the monsignor short of disaster.

"*Monsignore*, it's all measured off."

"But it can be remeasured," said the bishop. "Simply by lowering this, you get more."

Manzù had had enough.

"Just a minute," he said. "Nobody's lowering anything here except me and that can't be moved down one centimeter, not even half a centimeter."

This did not please the bishop, who replied haughtily.

"It was a suggestion to save waste on these doors which are so important for the Church and for the Holy Father."

"The only waste here is your time—and mine, *Monsignore*."

With that, Manzù clamped his mouth shut, and waited for them to leave. Capovilla and don Giuseppe hastily filled in with more words, describing the progress of the doors and assuring them all was going well. Finally, on the way out, Capovilla quietly apologized to Manzù.

"I know little about art," he said. "Except that only the artist should judge his work when it is being created."

"*Grazie.*"

"How are the busts coming?"

"Slowly. I'm not happy with them. I've put them aside for the doors."

"Would it help to see the Holy Father again?"

"Perhaps. Yes, perhaps it would."

"Fine. I'll tell him."

Capovilla phoned early the following Sunday.

"If you'd like to come over now, the Holy Father would be glad to see you. You can work on the portrait if you like, or else just have a chat with him."

"*Va bene*, I'll bring my tools and we can do a little of both."

Manzù prepared some fresh clay, grabbed his tools and headed for the Vatican in Capovilla's car which had been sent for him. This meeting was going to be without don Giuseppe and the sculptor immediately missed him. Had his friend told the Pope about the difficulty in portraying the dying Virgin? It might explain why he had been summoned so quickly.

Upon entering the papal library, Manzù found John dressed in dazzling pontifical robes and posing for Luigi Felici, the Vatican photographer. It was to be an official photograph and John wore the heavy tiara which he kept in his closet. He also was attired in a great silk cape worthy of an emperor, speckled with golden *fleurs de lis* and richly embroidered with all the symbols and saints of the papal office.

"Ah Manzù!" he said, calling him by the family name

as though they were two classmates, or fellow soldiers at the front. "Just whom we need. See if the folds of the cape go clear to the end."

Quite clearly, he did not trust the photographer to do much more than snap the picture—if that. He had inherited him, as he had everyone else in the papal court. He did not like having his picture taken, but this was another duty of his office and had to be done. John was kindly, as always. Contrary to his usual manner, however, he was nervous and let it be understood that he wanted to finish this quickly.

Floodlamps beamed in at him from all sides, removing all defining shadows. Manzù could visualize the final photo. It was going to be an official photograph which would make the subject look like a boiled and painted Easter egg, or an embalmed saint. It would be scattered in religious homes, store fronts, refectories and embassies around the world. It would be glanced at or prayed to by nuns and children, by whores and saints, by men before battle, by the dying and the victorious. It would be lit by candles, torn by infidels, and kissed by murmuring millions. It would be a mass-produced icon of our age.

Under the egg-shaped tiara, John's face and ears seemed massive and strangely naked, as though they had suddenly slipped down from the secret interior of the big golden egg. Sweat began to run down his temples and his soft brown eyes darted from side to side as if emerging from a tunnel. The camera began to click away, but not too successfully. Each time Felici clicked, John blinked. To remedy this, the photographer sought to alter his timing by snapping John after each blink. There ensued then a sort of dual between the Holy Father and the pontifical photographer—a game of beat the blink. Finally, John took a deep sigh and stared

150

ahead without blinking at all, but unfortunately at that moment the photographer ran out of film.

When it was over, John left the library while servants cleared out the lamps and equipment. He returned wearing his white soutane and the little *zucchetto*, to sit down in the usual chair by the window with a wan smile.

"Spot lights blind me," he said. "The Pope is supposed to lead his children, but when they include photographers, we are bound to have trouble. The day I came onto the balcony of St. Peter's, after being elected Pope, the many reflectors and lights in the piazza blinded me so that I saw nothing. There I stood—the new Pope before his flock, but unable to see them."

He paused and nodded with a chuckle.

"The soutane they had prepared in advance for the new Pope was so small I could hardly raise my arms. It seemed obvious from this that the tailors didn't want me. And since the people of Rome had not elected me their bishop, how could I know if they approved of me unless I looked at them? Yet there I was, blind as one staring into the sun."

Manzù smiled in return, and began to work on another bust—the fourth one. Capovilla sat in a far corner reading some papers, and there were no more interruptions. So the work went well. Occasionally, John would make a comment or two which would be followed by a long silence.

"I saw your name the other day. In the yearbook of the Ateneo di Bergamo."

"What was my name doing there?"

"They list you as an illustrious advisor."

It never failed to amaze Manzù that a man of such high office could enjoy the tiny details of small town life. Even more, that he could be pleased to discover the name of an acquaintance in an academic publication. Yet it so delighted the Pope that he sent for the book to point to the sculptor's name.

"Bergamo remembers you with affection," he said, his hand with the papal ring patting the page of the yearbook.

Manzù thought differently of Bergamo, but did not say it. Instead, he told the Pope of his project to give the city a large bronze sculpture of an artist and model to honor the great painter, Michelangelo da Caravaggio.

"The city plans to put the work in Piazza Mascheroni which will then be called Piazza Michelangelo da Caravaggio."

"But Lorenzo Mascheroni was a great mathematician," said Pope John, somewhat surprised. "Where will they put him?"

"There's going to be a new street with a new name, so the piazza will be changed, too."

"Mascheroni was a great genius," said the Pope. "He could solve impossible problems by using only a compass. They should keep a street or a piazza for him, too."

After a bit, he said: "Now that I'm no longer as poor as a country priest, I have been able to help the Seminary of Bergamo. It's not too far away from your piazza."

They talked then about trips they had taken, of Manzù's medals for the Olympic games which had pleased the Pope, and of art in general. John was especially indignant about the modern architecture used in churches and convents.

"They look like warehouses or grain silos," he said. "If I get dressed to celebrate the Lord, the place where I do this should be dressed up, too."

Manzù agreed that some modern churches were not very successful. Their ugly interiors left one feeling more lost than found. But this happened mostly with hideous imitations of traditional baroque or classic, and not with newly conceived works.

"Permit me to suggest, *Santità*, that current architecture is one of the most beautiful achievements of modern thought because it is designed to serve man and is created by men—artists and architects—who believe in what they are doing."

"And you, Manzù, in whom we have so much faith—how go the doors for this old church of ours?"

Manzù looked up to see if there was any sign that the Pope knew of his trouble. He found him staring out the window toward the façade of the basilica—as though, by lucky chance, the doors might have been put up for him overnight.

"Fine," said Manzù. "We are making progress."

John blinked and they did not pursue it further. Manzù would have liked to talk about how to portray Mary's death, but feared this might lead the Pope to propose a solution which he could not accept. So he said nothing and continued working until the end of the sitting. Upon leaving, however, he sensed that John actually did know of his trouble and had a solution for it. The sculptor did not ask, however, and never learned whether or not this was true.

But he did get an answer in an unexpected way at their next meeting three weeks later in early November. He had sent the Pope six plaster busts to choose from—four which had been done in the library, plus two others derived from those in his studio. They included one waist high with cape and mitre, which he did not especially like, but sent along anyway.

When Manzù arrived, Pope John was already looking at the work with Monsignor Capovilla. It was arranged with three busts in one row and three in another, so that John went up one row and down the other like a general with subordinates, peering into the unblinking faces of soldiers on review. Joining the group, Manzù felt uneasy. There was an odd sense of betrayal, as though he had abandoned his figures to a commander who knew little of their true weakness and strength.

After they had done this twice, John returned to stare at two busts—both showing the *camauro* hat low over his ears.

"How strange," he said. "These two remind me of my mother."

"Yes," he said, speaking directly to one of them. "She did look a little like you."

From the entire group, the Pope was supposed to select those which he favored most for casting into bronze and he picked the two which most resembled his mother. Manzù nodded without saying a word. He had some distinct reservations about this choice, however, and the Pope sensed it.

"Don't destroy any of the others," he said quickly. "Let's keep them all."

"Why?"

"Because we can use them. We will need each one."

"Excuse me, *Santità*, but if they are not pleasing to me or to you, they must be destroyed."

Manzù felt that at least three of them, maybe four, would have to be destroyed—including the one with the mitre. Nor was he too sure about one of those resembling the Pope's mother. So he had said he would destroy them. He saw nothing arrogant in taking such a position before any man, even a Pope. The same impulse which drives an artist to create a perfect work naturally leads him to destroy anything too far off the mark. Michelangelo destroyed all sketches in his possession before he died. The Pope seemed to understand this, for he changed the subject.

"I thought of you this morning. Someone asked me how we could answer all the questions which would be asked at the Vatican Council when the bishops came to Rome from around the world. I remembered the sculptor Manzù

154

saying he finds his answers as he works, in the work itself, and I said—'Never mind, *Monsignori*, we will find our answers as we work in the Council, or afterwards as we apply it to the world.' "

How, wondered Manzù, could the Pope think such things? With all the words of saints and doctors of the Church, why did he choose those of an untutored sculptor who never went beyond the third grade?

"And just as you helped us today, we want to be with you in your work, especially your work on the doors."

Did that mean he had heard about it from Capovilla? Did he know of the intrusion into his studio by the commission? Perhaps he even knew of the problem with Mary. Regardless, he was not going to force himself upon the artist.

"If you need us at any time, just call the Monsignor and we can see each other. The afternoons are always better."

Manzù mumbled his thanks and, as he began to kiss the papal ring in a gesture of respect and friendship, John drew him close, clasping his shoulder. It was the gesture of a father to his son, an embrace where more questions were asked and more answered than could ever be formed by words.

On the way home, across the piazza with its stone saints and then down through the dappled light along the river, the sculptor felt John's presence with him all the way. In his own fashion, the Pope had given his solution to the problems of the doors. It was an affectionate parting which drove Manzù forward—with a gentle reminder that he would find the answers in his hands as he worked.

mondi   prima prova d'autore

la guerra

Chapter Thirteen

Feeling John's invisible presence behind him, Manzù began work on the doors and slowly, inevitably, made them his own. He thought no more of the basilica of St. Peter's which was to eventually claim them. He thought only of a field of panels which became part of him. He dreamt of them at night and saw them at dawn. He worked without pause, dragging himself to bed only when he could do no more. The saints and the men and women, together with Christ and Mary, all dwelt with him, ate with him, slept in his bed. It was a separate private company and before it ended he felt they all knew one another quite well.

The problem of how to portray Mary reached a climax one morning after finishing the first paper layout of Christ on the Cross. He used paper cutouts before beginning with clay because it was easier and faster. This was done by cutting out the flat shape of figures to appear on the panel, then giving them to his assistant, Mauro, who would run up the ladder and attach them to their places on the panel. From below, Manzù could then study them— blue or red silhouettes against the white plaster—and so direct his assistant to move them about in order to obtain the proper spaces and voids.

157

Sculpture was created by such an alternation of figure and background, of form and no form, of substance and shadow—just as music was composed of notes interspersed with varying intervals of silence. Manzù often worked harder to create the silent intervals, the voids, than he did the spaces which were to be filled with sculpture. For as in music where the weight of silence can equal that of sound, so in sculpture do empty voids balance full forms.

On this morning, the studio floor was awash with discarded blue Christs trampled, torn, mixed in with differing versions of Adam and Eve. Fixed onto the top right panel were three figures which seemed to work best. Christ was nailed to the Cross, while Eve leaned in sorrow against its base and Adam witnessed the event with mute despair.

This created a triangle of three forms—Christ at the top, with Adam and Eve in the two bottom corners. It also created a problem in the adjacent panel with Mary, which now required a similar triangle or variant of it. Manzù began to solve this by placing Mary—dying alone—at the bottom of the panel. As soon as this was done, the balance of spaces and voids with the Christ panel required two other figures, two perpendiculars coming down onto the horizontal figure of Mary, preferably at a vector, so as to create a balancing triangular form.

Yet what figures could be used? The most obvious, as suggested by don Giuseppe, were angels descending to collect Mary for her bodily assumption into heaven. Manzù could not do this, however, for it was not convincing. He did not believe in angels. Nor did he believe in the Virgin's bodily assumption into heaven.

Despite this, he began to create two things which he called angels, for lack of a better word. They were descending forms which in reality were folds of cloth arched in a way that suggested there was life within them. To further this impression, he extended from one of them a forearm and a shank of windblown hair. From the other, there came an arm to touch Mary, and a face, also with hair blown in the wind. Yet these were only rippling folds of cloth, because beneath them there was nothing—no body or being. Manzù made them first in cardboard, soaked in a plaster solution, wrinkling it on the panel to suggest the flight of an empty form, or of wind made visible, and so indicating the spirit leaving the body as it drops toward the dark grave.

Don Giuseppe was very happy with these forms, though what they represented to him was different than what they meant to Manzù.

"Beautiful," he said. "You have created a beautiful concept of Mary's assumption into heaven."

"For you, maybe. Not for me."

"You have two angels taking her body and soul up toward heaven. They are going *up* because the angel's hair is blown *downward*."

"Those aren't angels. They are folds of cloth in the wind. There is no body inside the cloth."

"Doesn't matter," said don Giuseppe happily. "Angels don't have corporeal form. Hobbes claims they do, since an incorporeal substance is self-contradictory. But he was opposed by Locke, Aquinas and many more wiser men."

"What else do they know about angels, professor?"

"Lacking bodies, they are free of human passions and conflicts. And they are telepathic. One angel can pass its ideas to another simply by an act of will, without any exterior means of communication. Also, they don't need to talk. Knowing a basic principle, they can go straight to all its conclusions. So there is no need for rational discussion. They know it all . . . . "

"Sounds like an awfully dull life, unless you want to be a bad angel."

"Their travels must be fun. They go from one place

to another without traversing the intervening space, and without loss of time. They pop up wherever they want, like that—presto!—and they're on your doors."

Manzù smiled and don Giuseppe pretended to be shocked.

"Giacomo—you, a materialist, find this hard to believe? What about electrons in modern quantum mechanics? Don't they jump from outer to inner orbits of the atom without taking time or passing through inter-orbital space?"

"Marvelous," said the sculptor. "It proves I did not create any angels, because you can see mine in midflight. . ."

"Taking Mary up to heaven."

"No, *Monsignore*. This is the death of a woman—of Mary, or of all women. It is the moment when the spirit of life leaves the body."

"Except that Mary's body and soul went to heaven all together. Also, maybe she never died. Some theologians claim she did not have to die since she was without sin and therefore as immortal as Eve before eating the forbidden fruit. However, our second Eve was obedient to God and so became the mother of the second Adam. Don't you concede that your angels are moving toward heaven?"

Manzù shook his head and drank a glass of wine. They were having lunch in the studio. Before them loomed the doors with the crumpled cardboard forms of the angels hovering above Mary. It was a bright day in February, with a feel of returning spring. Inge or somebody had placed some mimosa on the base of a dancing nude which had been cast in bronze and was awaiting shipment.

"Giacomo, you have sent two angels to pick up Mary and now you say they have nowhere to go. That's like getting on a bus and saying it has no destination."

"Don't talk nonsense. All this has no relation with what

I have to do. It's nothing but fiction. What I'm interested in, is life and form."

There was more to it than that, but he did not know how to say it with words. True, he had created something without being aware beforehand of what he was doing. And now that it was done, he did not know what it all meant —or even if it had to have a meaning. But he did know what it was not, and also how he felt about Mary. Naturally, he differed with don Giuseppe.

"Mary is the Church," said the priest. "In her the Church is seen for the first time."

"I see her as a woman."

"The woman you see is the Church of the Old Covenant giving birth through Mary to the Messiah, and with him to the whole Church of the New Covenant—or Renewed Covenant. She is the link."

"Maybe, but the link I see is through her body—through the miracle of birth. That's the only miracle I can speak about, because it can be witnessed. It's the central miracle of human existence and it's contained in all women, before and after Mary."

"Yes, but the miracle working in Mary allows her to make the Son of God a member of the human race. So she is most blessed among all women."

"I don't know, or better, I can't line up all the thoughts on this which run around inside me. All that I can say about it is based on the human being, since it's impossible for me to accept your symbols. Most everyone sees his own mother as blessed among women and worthy of a miraculous love. So all these mothers are also links in the great chain of being, running from birth to death."

"Fine. That means your angels are custodians of the immortal matrix."

"Why must they do anything? Can't some angels just do nothing?"

"All right," said don Giuseppe. "But let's not tell anybody about it. They look awfully busy, doing just what they're supposed to do."

It went like that and they drank their wine and don Giuseppe began to read poetry. He often did and the sculptor enjoyed it. But on this day it was difficult to concentrate because Manzù suddenly realized that the panel with Mary was now so filled with movement that the Crucifixion panel appeared to be static. The figure would have to be taken off the Cross and moved into a Deposition—perhaps with a rope as he had used in earlier works.

By using a rope, one man could lower Christ. Otherwise, too many figures would be required. Also with a rope, Christ could remain suspended near to where he met his death—a single column of a man who crossed the gap crying out to his God in a loud voice. Once lowered to the ground, he becomes possessed by the living and a subject for pity, prayer and adoration. But while still on the Cross, he is also a subject for anger and outrage against those who would so kill him. Certainly no one witnessing a man strung up could ever forget it. One morning in April during the war, Manzù had come upon a young partisan fighter strung up by his feet from the outside beam of a farmhouse . . .

> *Sylvia, do you remember still*
> *that season of your mortal life*
> *when beauty brightened*
> *your laughing and elusive eyes*
> *and joyous and wistful you rose*
> *to the brink of youth?*

Don Giuseppe was reading Leopardi's *Sylvia*. It had

little to do with Manzù's trend of thought, but he sought to listen to it anyway.

> *I'd watch the clear sky,*
> *the golden lanes and gardens,*
> *the mountains there and the far sea.*
> *No mortal tongue can tell*
> *what I felt then.*

. . . the partisan was naked, with only a torn undershirt caught around his chest. His body seemed very white against the red farmhouse wall—except for the black nimbus of pubic hair where his scrotum hung down against his belly with the inert weight of overripe fruit. Most startling of all were the dangling arms, outstretched as though appealing to the ground to open up and take him as he was.

Legs that once walked the fields, hands that pruned peach limbs, a loin that knew another's warmth, a mouth that enriched wisdom with laughter, and eyes that blinked up at the sky—all of it hung there in a shocking column of silence. It was not safe to stay and stare. Yet he could not leave and so lingered on, as in an empty theater where the audience had fled in fright before such a hideous crime— begging now to be swallowed up by the earth which refused it. For the sin was too monstrous to be buried. It would remain to haunt the land, as it did now his memory. . .

> *Oh, how sudden are you gone,*
> *gone, companion of my young prime,*
> *my wept-for hope!*
> *Is our world this? these*
> *the tasks, delights, longing, and occasions*
> *which we shared in talk so often?*
> *Is this the doom of mankind?*

163

. . . this was not only the murder of a farm boy who refused to run from tyranny. It was a sacrifice of one more redeemer of man. He had run the race at Thermopylae and ridden horseback through the night to Lexington. He had fallen at Legnano, Dunkirk and by the bloody Ebro. He had sailed the Santa Maria and soared at Kitty Hawk. He had offered his body to yellow fever and lain on his back for three years to paint the Sistine Chapel. He had split the atom, and soared the skies, and died on a launching pad with fire in his lungs. His voice had rung out in the English Commons for the rights of man, in Virginia for liberty or death, and across a clumsy cable from Baltimore to Washington he had exclaimed with dots and dashes: "What hath God wrought!"

So on an April morning, before a farmhouse near Bergamo, a youth hung upside down in honor, rather than walk upright in shame. Such were these—the elite among men, the true sons of God. There was about all of them a particular aura, so that when you saw one of them on a Cross, or hung from a beam, you could only say: "Here passed the race of man. Here are footsteps in the sky."

> *At the sight of truth, you fell,*
> *Unfortunate one, your hand pointed to distant*
> *Cold death and a bare tomb.*

With these last lines, a strange note crept in don Giuseppe's voice. Manzù looked at his friend and saw him, with the opened book in his lap, appearing quite sad. He had never seen don Giuseppe like this and it alarmed him.

"Old friend, what's wrong?"

"Nothing, Giacomo."

"You're sad . . . what touched you?"

"This poem is beautiful."

There was more to it than that, but he did not pursue

it. He said no more that day and soon forgot about it as he began work on the new panel showing Christ in descent from the Cross.

He did the figure being lowered by a rope held by one man. This was Adam for don Giuseppe, but for Manzù he was any man. A woman, who could be Eve or any woman, leaned in one corner against the Cross. This retained a triangular arrangement in each panel, and at the same time made a circular link with the panel of Mary. One half of the circle was formed by the arc of the top angel running through the head of the second angel and thence to Mary who points to the second half, starting with Adam and going up the rope to Christ, whose inclined head leads back to the top angel.

Among the slashes in the background, done with a sketching knife, there was a circular one above the head of Christ. But there were no wounds in the hands or feet or side.

"What about the stigmata?" asked don Giuseppe.

"Oh no, we leave them aside."

The priest thought about this for a moment.

"Well, they eventually did heal. So you could say it's a question of how long it took—which nobody knows. But I wonder what the commission will say."

They learned about the commission's feelings, and a bit more, a few weeks later when Cardinal Testa came with two monsignori. The prelate said nothing about the missing wounds, however, probably because he was so overwhelmed by the whole composition of Christ being lowered from the Cross.

"It's very strong," he said.

Manzù blinked and waited in silence.

"It's too strong," he said. "Too tragic."

The sculptor still said nothing.

"It's too shocking," added one monsignore.

"I'm afraid it's too painful," said the other monsignore.

All three men then looked at Manzù, as if expecting him to answer for the death of Christ.

"What do you want me to do about it?"

"He looks too dead," said the first monsignore.

"*Porca miseria!*" cried the sculptor. "He *is* dead. He died on the Cross, didn't he? What do you want me to do about that?"

For a moment the three clerics considered what could be done.

"Maybe something less dramatic," said Testa.

"Just a minute, monsignori," said don Giuseppe. "May I remind you that Manzù is not responsible for the Crucifixion of Our Lord?"

"We know that," said Testa. "It's just the way he is recreating it."

"He is bearing witness to the sacred event," said de Luca firmly, "just as you and I bear witness to Christ. And how can you expect a true witness to play down the drama and reality of Christ's sacrifice—especially in an age where there is growing skepticism that it ever happened?"

Manzù suppressed a smile. Bravo for don Giuseppe, giving them hell by the book. It stopped them in their tracks —but not for long. Testa quickly rallied with a fresh attack.

"Where are the words?"

"What words?"

"The Latin text beneath the panels, describing what is happening."

Again don Giuseppe rose to head off the cardinal.

"Do we need any words here, Eminence? What is happening seems fairly obvious, no?"

"Maybe here, but when you get to the other panels you will need to make clear the moral of each death."

"How clear? Who reads Latin?"

"Latin," said Testa flatly, "is the universal and living language of the Church."

For a moment everyone considered this while staring at the figures of the Virgin and Christ whose language was Aramaic. Finally Manzù felt it was the moment to make clear his position.

"I'm sorry, but I don't feel the need for words in any language."

"Just the same, Manzù, you will find you are going to need them."

The cardinal seemed very sure of what he said. He held onto his golden pectoral cross with one hand while inserting four pudgy fingers of the other between the buttons of his black cassock. So he stood, hanging onto a cross and onto his buttons, while staring fixedly at the sculptor from folds of facial fat — a rude form of pressure which Manzù specifically disliked. Before he could reply, however, don Giuseppe stepped behind the old man and the two monsignori and made a sign for the sculptor to agree with them.

Manzù nodded in a general way and said no more. When the cardinal had gone, he asked don Giuseppe what this had meant.

"I can't insert words onto these panels," he said. "This isn't a comic strip."

"Don't worry. These men are so old, they forget. Your best practice with them is to always say 'yes' — and then do as you like. Besides, you would never be able to use any of Testa's Latin texts."

"How so?"

"Because he doesn't know Latin that well."

Unfortunately, Cardinal Testa had a memory like an elephant and soon behaved like one. As work began on the lower panels, he came to Manzù's studio with the massive and insensitive arrogance of an inspector general. Not even Pope Julius II—God's terrible vicar and the autocratic benefactor of Michelangelo—would have dared to so rudely invade the privacy of creation. Testa's sallies were further complicated by his ignorance of art. Pope John suffered from a similar lack, but he openly admitted it and respected the artist—while Testa did not.

So the cardinal had no critical right to speak. Even more shocking, he had no legal right—though hardly anyone knew this at the time. The will of the Bavarian prince, in providing money for the doors, specified that the artist should be left free to execute his work without interference. The wording of the testament indicates the prince expected that some monsignori would inevitably seek to dictate to the artist at work:

"Upon obtaining the commission, the artist will be sovereign in the execution of the work, in both artistic and technical sense. Neither the Commision, nor the single members will have the right to exercise any influence whatsoever on the artistic and technical execution of the work, though the Commission will have the right and the duty to continually oversee the financial aspects. This control nevertheless must limit itself strictly to the financial side or to the use of available means, and must not be abused by influencing the artist in aesthetic and technical questions."

To its shame and disgrace, the Vatican commission for the doors never told Manzù about this—nor did they inform Monsignor Capovilla, thereby depriving him of his duty of referring it in turn to Pope John. It was kept a secret by a few men. The commission's astonishing maneuvers did not end there, and should be set down for the history of this devious affair.

The testament specified that the German ambassador to the Holy See should be appointed as a member of the commission for the doors, where he was to also take part in the jury selecting the sculptors. But the Vatican commission never informed the German envoy of his rights and, to his chagrin and sorrow, he learned of this only by accident in March, 1960. Applying for clarification, he received a letter advising him of his rights to be part of the commission—but he learned of this only after the jury had picked three Italians from an international competition. Similarly, Prince Konrad, brother of the deceased Prince Georg, was supposed to be on the commission. Unlike the German ambassador, he knew his rights. But the old man was able to do nothing about it, since he was never called to Rome.

Because of delays in erecting the doors, the revived German naval academy began to demand its right to the unused fortune, some $200,000. It obtained almost two-thirds of this sum after a Munich court battle in which there was little chance for the Holy See to display the highest of Christian virtues: charity. With so much money taken from it, the Vatican complained bitterly to Prince Konrad who made up the difference from his own estate—a private act of generosity which was also never made public.

Unaware of his legal rights, Manzù did not dare turn Cardinal Testa away from his door. Also the cardinal came on an ambiguous passport, having been personally asked by Pope John to "stand by" in case of need. John had meant him to stand by in silence. The cardinal, however, saw no reason to keep silent at any time.

Most of his interventions were based upon a concept that art either must club people over the head or trap them by stealth. One day he inspected the panel on death in space—a figure tumbling through a void, its mouth open in anguish.

"Is this a man or a woman?" he asked.

"It could be either," replied Manzù.

"It's in the sky?"

"More or less."

"Then you should have an airplane. Perhaps in the upper corner.

"Why?"

"To show it's in the sky. That this person, man or woman or what have you, is falling from an airplane."

"Maybe it isn't an airplane. Maybe it's a space ship."

"All right. Then the nose of a spaceship."

"Maybe it isn't a spaceship. Maybe it's in a circus and this is an acrobat falling from a broken trapeze."

This variety of possibilities did not please the cardinal. He shook his head, as if to free it of buzzing flies.

"If you don't show a wing or a space craft, or even a busted trapeze, nobody will know where this person is tumbling from. All they will see is somebody tumbling about . . . just tumbling from nowhere."

That was exactly what Manzù wanted—tumbling from nowhere, or anywhere. Death in space could happen on earth, as in heaven. A person could go tumbling like that through life, with both feet on the ground. It could even happen in the Roman Curia, with a pectoral cross on the belly.

"You understand what I am saying?"

The sculptor nodded mutely, as don Giuseppe had instructed him, then turned to work on the other panels. But Testa never forgot what he wanted and kept after it. When he saw the death of St. Stephen, he again asked that it be inscribed with a Latin text, such as: "I SAW THE HEAVENS OPEN AND CHRIST AT THE SIDE OF HIS FATHER."

Manzù had worked quite hard on this one, casting three bronzes before getting what he wanted. Any wording would blunt its thrust. This was the first Christian martyr stoned to death. The figure was less saint than man, however, and it could have been any man being stoned to death by a mob, or by an unseen assailant.

In a similar way, Testa wanted words explaining the death of Gregory VII—the famous ones attributed to him: "I HAVE LOVED JUSTICE AND HATED INIQUITY, THERE-FORE I DIE IN EXILE." Manzù felt this was also unneces-sary, because he had said it in the work itself. The brute phy-sical power of the standing figure of Robert Guiscard, wear-ing a German helmet, looms over the dying Pope whose spirit flickers on within a feeble body. Also, it did not have to be only Pope Gregory. It could have been Thomas Becket, murdered in his own cathedral by the knights of Henry II, or Dietrick Bonhoeffer dying in a Nazi concentration camp. For this reason, as well as for aesthetic reasons, Manzù did not want restricting words. In this and in all the other panels, his desire was for the work to speak to as many people as possible. Testa, on the other hand, feared that broad themes would hatch heresy—such as the possibility that God might not be a Catholic, or that death would snatch someone away before he had said the proper number of Hail Marys.

When he saw Death on Earth, with the stricken woman in a back-tilting chair at the sudden moment of death, and a child screaming from the widow, Testa wanted to make clear that this tragedy was happening to an obedient Catholic.

"This should be a religious death," he said.

"How religious?"

"You should put some prayer beads in the hands of that woman."

"But why?"

"To show that she is Catholic."

Up to this point Manzù had followed the advice of don Giuseppe and avoided any direct refusal. But this was too much. The panel had been created with Inge in mind and the terrorized child in the window was his own little Giulia. It had been difficult and painful and, of all the panels, it was closest to him. Yet now this cardinal had entered into the imagined death of a woman Manzù loved—with the intention of thrusting prayer beads into her lifeless hands.

"No," he replied. "I do not think we need them."

"I see a small cross and a few beads here," he said, indicating the hand which had fallen without life to the floor.

Manzù shook his head.

"I don't hold your ideas," he said. "This is death, the tragedy of death, and that tragedy doesn't belong to priests or to rosary beads because death makes no concessions, even for those who don't die in bed."

Testa appeared to sense that he had invaded the privacy of the sculptor's life, for he quickly withdrew. But he did not give up so easily on the Cain and Abel panel which brought them finally to the breaking point.

To describe mankind's first murder, Manzù drew upon his memory of a fight he had seen in Naples. It was a violent and frightening battle, with all the insane substance of fratricide. He came upon it in a side street: two young men beating each other with such fury that even those watching it were without the courage to step in and stop it.

It was a sickening spectacle. No words came from the two youths who were past the point of insult or curse. There was only the sound of their gasping breath, their desperate grunting, and the thudding of fists against flesh. Finally they grappled and fell to the street, the smaller youth hitting his head on the cobblestones with a dull thud of a bursting melon. One word came from him, more a moan than a cry: "Enough!"

Despite this, Cain continued to beat the head of his brother—thump, thump, thump—until one woman echoed his plea in a scream: "Enough! Enough! You're killing him!"

Finally several bystanders threw themselves upon Cain to separate him from his crime. Manzù remembered the young man's eyes filled with terror at what he saw on the pavement. Yet even more fixed in memory was the sound of the head being beaten—the cracked chamber of life and dreams, the house of hope and fear and love crying *"Enough! Enough!"*—all in one long moan, followed by *thump, thump, thump*, into the dark pit of death.

He did this panel with Cain standing, dressed in pants and open shirt as he brains his brother. Abel, crumpled between Cain's legs, is defenseless and naked. Manzù liked it, but Cardinal Testa immediately suspected it had a dangerous significance.

"Why is one dressed and the other not?"

"Abel is the shepherd and pure of spirit. So he is naked, as was Adam in the Garden. The other, his murderer, is not pure. So he wears clothes, as did Adam afterwards."

"Why does he wear modern clothes?"

"Because fratricide has sadly continued, and this sculpture should speak to the people of our time."

"It looks like an allegory on class warfare," said the cardinal. "An industrialist is beating up a worker."

"It could be that, if Your Eminence sees it that way."

"Well, that's wrong."

"Eminence, don't suppose too much. I use only the language of form, and would like what I represent to pertain to everyone. Certainly this isn't nice to look at. But we're condemning it, not approving. Murder is born and dies with man. It's tragic, but neither religion nor class struggle can alter it."

"You can't do that. This is a political statement. It can be seen as a capitalist beating up a union organizer. You can't say that."

"I'm not saying that exactly. I don't imagine the worker's drama when I work. Besides, every Pope in the last sixty years has talked of the exploitation of workers and their rights. And we've had the great revolution. But here I only want to make a sculpture. So keep your fears to yourself, since there's no reason for them."

"No," said the cardinal flatly. "We cannot accept this. It will help the communists and hurt the Church."

"And what do you propose?"

"Put them in clothes which they must have worn at the time—animal skins. Both of them. And give Cain a club or the jaw bone of an ass to hit his brother."

"Come now, I beg you to have a little respect. Are you asking me to make trinket saints? I'm concerned with life and naturally with the life I live."

Testa left very upset. Shortly thereafter, he proposed a compromise.

"If you can't do it with animal skins, then dress Abel in the same modern clothes as his brother. That will eliminate the suggestion of class warfare."

Manzù did not want to do it. But he did not want to break over this issue and so stop the cycle of work which had become intense. As he considered this, Testa made a final proposition.

"Look, Manzù. I'll accept everything you have done, if you'll agree to change this one panel."

"All right, I'll try. I don't know how well it will come out, or if I can do it. But I will try."

He did a new panel with both brothers dressed alike, and Testa was pleased. But when Manzù saw it after it had been cast in Milan, he felt like a thief. This did not belong on his doors. So he eliminated it and cast the other model with the naked Abel, fixing it onto the door. When Cardinal Testa saw this, he was quite disturbed.

"No, no, this is wrong. We were in agreement. You

promised to put up both Cain and Abel with clothes on."

"I'm sorry, I tried it but it doesn't work. Only this one pleases me. So it must go on the door. If you want to take it off, do it and we'll have a hole there. I will not do it over again."

The cardinal stomped out, very angry.

Manzù knew then that the time had come for him to speak to Pope John and so get this general of the Church off his back, or give up the doors. But before that happened —indeed, before he reached this bitter breaking point with Testa—something else occurred which altered the face of the doors, as well as the life of Giacomo Manzù.

Chapter Fourteen

ONE night in March Manzù awakened from a dream in which Monsignor de Luca was dead. By the time he had assured himself it was not true, he was fully awake and staring at the ceiling. When he closed his eyes, he saw don Giuseppe again—stretched out in bed, wearing his pompom hat, his hands folded together clasping a rosary, his face the violet hue of death.

The sculptor looked at the ceiling and told himself it was nothing. Dreams needed to be interpreted by experts. They were visible flags of hidden regiments at battle. This dream was a sign of anxiety to finish the doors and of need for his friend. Without him, the battle with Testa would be lost. Don Giuseppe's death would be his own. *Porca miseria,* how sad. But even then, he would never give up. He would take the doors with him into his own tomb and finish them there. Thinking this, Manzù rolled over and went to sleep.

The next morning Inge came into his studio and he could see from her eyes that an island in their lives was sinking beneath the sea.

"They took him to the hospital last night."

"What happened?"

"Oh, Giacomo, you saw it in your dream—will he die?"

"What happened, Inge?"

"Nucia said he had to be operated on for his stomach pains. She said they were doing it now."

"*Porco cane.* It can't be true."

Yet he knew it was. Don Giuseppe had suffered from stomach pains for a long time—about two years. He drank less and less wine. He gave up smoking. But he refused to do much more. His sister, Nucia, tried to have him examined properly, and Pope John's doctor also suggested X-rays. But the priest had avoided any such final encounter.

It was more important to meet with Pope John, or Palmiro Togliatti or any one of several hundred other men and women to whom he had become a silent witness and a personal friend. It was better to serve an old age home, a children's orphanage, argue with the world's literary great, counsel artists and run a publishing house whose emblem was an obelisk and fish and rising sun. It was better to plunge forward and offer the living world a home between your hands, or a seat on the threshold of your heart. It was better to go it all the way in life—occupying all of your living space—rather than pull back to save yourself. You owed to your neighbor not what you could, but what you should. Only in that way could you be fair to yourself.

So it was that a few hours before they wheeled him into the operating room at the Fatebenefratelli hospital, don Giuseppe dashed off four lines to Capovilla, seeking to calm any fears his friends might have, adding "I have been a sinner and an *outsider*; but I loved Jesus, the Church, my priesthood. . . the Pope." And so it was that they found an untended cancer within him, the size of a grapefruit.

The operation seemed a success. Within a few days, it was said, the monsignor would be able to receive visitors. But other trouble developed in his lungs and his doctors became alarmed. This information quickly reached

Pope John who immediately got into his car and drove to the hospital. It is located on the Tiberina, the island in the Tiber, and John took the same route across St. Peter's Square and down along the river which don Giuseppe and Manzù had taken so many times together.

At the hospital there was hardly time to prepare for the Pope's arrival. On the fourth floor, where the priest lay in a corner room, there was a buzz of voices that the Pope was coming. Then the elevator door opened and he appeared, wrapped in a red cloak trimmed with gold braid, topped by a broad brimmed red hat and, in the middle of it all, his smiling face. Stepping into the corridor, he took off his hat, and, in so doing, opened the cloak to reveal a white soutane and a small gold pectoral cross. Behind him came Monsignor Capovilla.

In a room at the end of the corridor, don Giuseppe's doctor, Adriano Ossicini, hastily sought to ready the weakened priest for the arrival of his friend.

"It's not possible that he is coming here to see me," said don Giuseppe.

"What's this I hear?" asked Pope John, entering the little room. Going to the bedside, he patted don Giuseppe on the cheek and said again: "What were you saying?"

"*Santo Padre*, how is it that you have come here to see me?"

John pretended to be shocked.

"These Christians! What can we do with them? Where do they get their weird ideas? And why shouldn't I come to you? Isn't that my function—to come and testify to Christ, to serve you as a witness? *Ecce sacerdos.*"

"But you have so much to do."

"More important than this? Hardly—it's the heart of the priesthood. Or would you deny it to me?"

179

Don Giuseppe murmured something indistinct. He had trouble breathing and a fever, so it was difficult to speak. Even the Pope, who bent low over his friend, could hardly hear him. When John finally looked up at the waiting doctor, his eyes revealed the sorrow of what he had seen.

"How is he, doctor? Better, no?"

"Tell him," murmured don Giuseppe. "Tell him the truth."

Dr. Ossicini gave the Pope a rapid summary. After this, both he and Capovilla left the room and John remained alone with his friend. When they returned a quarter of an hour later, the Pope was preparing to leave.

"I must go now," he said. "We will keep in touch by phone."

"*Santità*, I'm overcome."

"Well, I'm not. The only way for me to be overcome is for you to get well."

Don Giuseppe nodded feebly and with such apparent sadness that John realized this remarkable man and priest was truly slipping away from sight. So he came again to his side and took his hand, as though this might hold him back.

"It's not so much the work on the Council as being alone at this moment. I have need of you, dear friend. I need to talk to you."

Don Giuseppe's eyes filled with tears and the Pope began to blink more than usual.

"I'm alone without people like you," he said, bending low over the bed to embrace the priest. Then he turned to go, only to stop.

"My hat," he said. "Where's my hat?"

Capovilla handed it to him.

"How humiliating for a Pope—someone has to carry his hat!"

Don Giuseppe smiled.

"You remember," he said, with some effort, "how I always said you would be Pope?"

"And how," said John "I called you a false prophet?"

Both men thought of this, and their earlier days. Then John said goodbye again and left, no longer able to hold back his tears.

After John had gone, don Giuseppe seemed to pick up strength. He spoke to nurses and doctors about the meeting, including something of his private talk with John, in which he apologized for falling ill when he was needed to organize television and radio coverage of the approaching Vatican Council.

"Don't worry," replied the Pope. "This Council is so important that whatever we do will not be equal to it."

Don Giuseppe said this was all the more reason for everyone to be on hand and do as much as possible.

"Yes, yes," said John. "The Catholic world is moving very fast. The important thing is to open a dialogue so that Rome can catch up with everybody else."

Don Giuseppe also recalled the Pope saying: "We will go far beyond the program — and this is to be expected if we keep it open, because it will reveal the living Church. We who wanted this Council are few; but in the end, many will be moved by it."

After recalling these words to those around him, don Giuseppe said, "Those who oppose the spirit of the Council will always be among us. It's sad, but true. Now they will begin to say that the Pope did not know what he was doing, that he opened a Pandora's box. They will call him the *papa buono*, the good Pope, meaning to imply that he was good but politically unwise. But we know this is not true and it will not stop us or the Council."

Although they let no one see don Giuseppe during the first days of his illness, Manzù went to the hospital every day, thinking maybe his friend would feel better and want to talk to somebody. The sculptor did not recall weeping at the death of his mother or father or his two brothers, but this was something else again. It was tearing him apart inside. He could not sleep and he could not work.

So when the time came to visit don Giuseppe, Manzù was exhausted. He drove with Inge to the island hospital as one climbs a mountain—doing it by steps, but with few words.

"He never told anybody about it," said Inge.

This was true. He had concealed his illness, if he was aware he had it. And he must have suspected something. There was, for example, his unexplained sadness the day he read *Sylvia*.

"Did he say anything about it to you—did you know?"

"No."

"He was always so sensitive about us, he never made you feel like an outsider."

Manzù said nothing.

"Giacomo?"

"Yes?"

"I loved that man. He was our friend."

"Yes, Inge, yes."

"Do you know what I mean?"

"Yes, Inge, yes."

As hospitals go, the Fatebenefratelli is pleasant enough. The river flows on both sides, there are tall pines, and the air is free of traffic fumes. Inside it is agreeable, too, without the usual odor of medicine and flowers, or the usual sense of grief and pain. The Brothers of St. John of God, who run the institution, wear white uniforms over their black robes and smile in a friendly and easy way. So it was not too difficult upon entering.

It became a different matter, however, when Manzù

reached the fourth floor with Inge and began to walk down the corridor toward the priest's room. The sculptor had a feeling that this would be the last time he saw his friend alive. So each step became more difficult and when they reached door 22, he could not bring himself to open it. As they stood there, a nurse suddenly emerged and held the door open, bidding them enter.

It was a blue room with a blue bed, and in it don Giuseppe seemed almost dead. He had his glasses off and his eyes were closed. Yet he heard them enter.

"Giacomo?" he said, keeping his eyes closed.

"Here we are!" said Manzù, his voice hollow.

"*Caro* Giacomo, you must pray for me."

Their island was indeed sinking. All that remained was a sunken face, the closed eyes and pale hands upon a blue bedcover. *Porca miseria*, he thought, death should not do this. It was indecent, and it had to be stopped. It had to be beaten back with everything possible, with those oxygen tanks in the corner, the medicines on the table, the new miracle drugs from America and the Soviet Union— everything, even their bare fists.

Next to the table lamp lay a Roman missal, a black rosary, and the silver crucifix Manzù had last seen in the priest's bedroom at Via delle Sette Sale—a simple crucifix he had brought with him as a youth from Lucania where he was born sixty-four years ago. These were the instruments which made death acceptable. "*Veni, Domine Jesù, noli tardare!*"

"Giacomo, you must pray for me."

Pray for him—how could he ask that? And yet what was more natural? Manzù looked back at the face to find don Giuseppe staring at him with the beginning of a slightly mischievous smile.

"Giacomo, you hear me—or are you deaf?"

An old lion, thought Manzù, a lion who would never give up.

"Forgive me, don Giuseppe, but you know how it is with me. I don't have to tell you that I can't do these things. You know that. Besides, it would be bad for you."

The priest's dark brown eyes opened even wider.

"You lazy hunk, even if you don't believe, you must say some prayers. They'll be the only ones heard. Up there . . . nobody listens to those who pray all the time."

"All right," said Manzù. "Tonight."

Don Giuseppe smiled.

"Who knows?" he said. "You might even come around to admitting the existence of angels."

"Ah . . . *sì.*"

Talking seemed to exhaust him and after a bit the priest again closed his eyes. A nurse said it was time for his medicine and asked the two visitors to wait outside.

"Don't go away, Giacomo."

"No, no."

"You will finish the doors?"

"Of course, with your help."

"No," he said, shaking his head.

"Then it can't be done. You must be there."

Somebody had to help him fight off death. Before he went through the black curtain, somebody had to take his hand and pull him back. Someone had to shout at him, calling him by name, saying he was needed on this side so that he would not hear the words from the other side: *"Veni, Domini, Jesù . . ."*

The nurse again suggested they go out. So they waited in the corridor until the doctor came and said he had given the monsignor an injection and it was better that he sleep for a while. Manzù asked what to expect and the doctor shook his head. He did not know.

So they left, and that evening Inge prayed for don Giuseppe. Manzù tried, but could not do it. He began to say, "O, *Signore* . . ." but got no further. It seemed dishonest to say something he did not believe. So he sat there and fumbled with his fingers and thought: "Get well, don Giuseppe, you are an island in our lives, don't sink, don't go, hold on and we will hold on to you . . ."

Yet even in this, Manzù was not able to help his friend. Don Giuseppe sank still further and all visitors were turned back, including those who just wanted to hold his hand. So it happened that late at night the priest found himself alone with Dr. Ossicini.

"Keep me company tonight," he said. "I don't ask you as a doctor, but as a friend. I'm too ill to sleep and too tired to talk. The medicine does not protect me from silence, but friendship does.

The doctor sat down with his old friend and shortly after midnight they came to give more medication.

"What time is it?"

"Past midnight, don Giuseppe. Today is the nineteenth of March. The day of St. Joseph—your namesake's day."

"Some feast day," said don Giuseppe. "I'll celebrate it by going to my Maker."

And so he did, two hours later.

The living who show up at a funeral reveal a great deal about the life of the person being buried. At don Giuseppe's, they were of all classes and ages—cardinals, artists, politicians, journalists, poets, actors, workmen, and even a group of orphans. The Pope sent a telegram and Togliatti sent roses. Ministers of government sat next to bitter enemies. Bishops said Amen with atheists. It was an immense testimonial to an immense man and in the middle of it all Manzù wondered how don Giuseppe found time for so many lives. How large was his heart to have been able to take so many into its chambers?

Inside the church of Santa Maria in Trastevere, Manzù and Inge sat off to the right with the black draped coffin in the center aisle. Looking over it, they could see several cardinals in scarlet, including Testa. Manzù watched him, aware the cardinal must have known what Monsignor de Luca thought of him. So it was generous of him to have come. Christian penance, perhaps, or maybe a suggestion from Pope John.

From time to time, Testa stared up at the mosaic in the apse figuring a row of large white sheep, symbols of the disciples. They were delightful, in a primitive way, with donkey heads and wolf tails. The cardinal did not seem to approve of them, though, and Manzù imagined him stomping into a twelfth century mosaicist crying: "Master, for shame! Your sheep have wolf tails and the heads of asses —are these lambs of the Lord? Do you want to dishonor the Holy Roman Apostolic Church and open its gates to foreign infidels?"

Manzù sighed, heavy with premonition. Now with don Giuseppe gone, how was he going to cope with such massive insensitivity? He was permanently exposed to the cardinal and to meddling members of the commission. One of its officials, Bishop Giovanni Fallani, had already approached him, saying, "Now that don Giuseppe is no longer, we will be seeing each other more frequently." Turning away from the bishop, Manzù had replied, "No, we won't, because don Giuseppe is irreplaceable!" That, of course, did not help matters, either. Manzù sighed again.

The Mass had begun, but rather than listen to it and stare at Testa across the coffin of don Giuseppe, he looked down at the floor and at a fallen pamphlet with the name of Teilhard de Chardin. Don Giuseppe had often spoken of this remarkable French Jesuit, who had suffered from senseless persecution by the Holy Office. The publication was stuck under the leg of the chair ahead, but its title was legible: "The Two Sides of the World." Wondering what two sides, Manzù wiggled it free and found within the text: " . . . the grand phenomenon which we are now witnessing represents a new and possibly final division of Mankind, based no longer on wealth but belief in progress. The old Marxist conflict between producers and exploiters becomes outdated—at the best, a misplaced approximation. What finally divides the men of today into two camps is not class but an attitude of mind—the spirit of movement.

"On the one hand, there are those who simply wish to make the world a comfortable dwelling-place; on the other hand, those who can only conceive of it as a machine for progress—or, better, an organism that is progressing.

"On the one hand, the 'bourgeois spirit' in its essence, and on the other the true 'toilers of the Earth', those of whom we may safely predict that, without violence or hatred, simply by biological predominance, will tomorrow constitute the human race.

"On the one hand, the cast-offs; on the other the agents and elements of planetisation . . .

"There is no name yet for this new element. We might call it *homo progressivus*, that is to say, the man to whom the terrestrial future matters more than the present. His emergence is clearly related to some new development in the thinking envelope of the earth—the Noosphere . . ."

"*Orate, fratres . . .*"

At the altar, the priest had shuffled about to face the assembly.

"Pray, brethren, that my sacrifice and yours may be acceptable to God the Father Almighty."

And Manzù thought:

—Pray, brethren, pray if you can. Pray that your sacrifices can be counted. Or even seen. It takes more than a wafer in the mouth, or six million Hail Marys. So pray for yourselves and don't bother about praying for the sacrifice of don Giuseppe. That's been accepted already. It lies in the hearts of everybody here. It lies in me. And it lies in that black box.

You must pray for me, Giacomo.

—Good-bye, dear don Giuseppe.

You hear me, Giacomo?

—True toiler of the earth, agent of planetisation, *homo progressivus*, first citizen of Noosphere . . . good-bye.

Up there, nobody listens to those who pray all the time.

—Nor to anyone, don Giuseppe. Good-bye, dear friend.

Inge saw Manzù trembling and took his hand. When the service was over, they could not bear to follow the coffin to the cemetery, and went directly home. After a glass of wine, Manzù decided to draw don Giuseppe from memory. It went rather well. Some of the sketches were better than those done when he was alive. There had always been trouble drawing him, just as there was difficulty doing the portrait of John.

Some time later, Mario returned with Mauro from the trip to the cemetery. They were both upset.

"They didn't bury him in a grave," said Mario.

"No? Where'd they put him?"

"In a wall crypt. His grave isn't ready. So they put him in the wall."

That was what prayers got you. All of Rome came to see him in the church. Then they hauled him away and shoved him into a hole in the wall.

"There's no name on it."

"No name on what?"

"Where they put him. Just a slab of cement over the

hole in the wall. It's the fourth up from the bottom. But nobody's going to find him when they come there, because his name isn't on it."

"Not even a name? They buried him without a name?"

"They probably figure this is only temporary. But his friends will not find him."

"*Mamma mia*, where are my paints?"

He took a board and began to draw the name in script lettering—*Giuseppe De Luca*. He drew it in red and embossed it with elegant capitals and flourishing letters. He did one he did not like and threw it away and started another. Mario and Mauro watched.

"He was also a monsignor," said Manzù. "We have to put that on, too."

"Monsignor," they repeated.

So he drew that as well, and gave it to Mario to put up because he could not stand to go and look at such a cement wall.

Then he sat down and began to draw again. He could not pray for him. He could not follow him into heaven or even to the Noosphere. But he could stand with him on earth. He could design his tomb. He could put his portrait on the doors of St. Peter's. And he could also stamp onto the doors for all generations to come, for as long as the doors hung on that church or remained visible to man: *To Don Giuseppe de Luca these doors of death are dedicated* . . . .

Chapter Fifteen

AFTER the departure of don Giuseppe, it was inevitable that Pope John and Manzù would draw closer to one another. But the sculptor was not prepared for what happened one month later when he returned to the papal library to find John at his desk reading from a large Bible.

"Manzù! You've come in time to hear a beautiful psalm!"

"Ah, yes?"

"Yes, *beati immaculati in via, qui ambulant in lege Domini . . .* "

"Santo Padre . . . " said Capovilla.

"*Qui scrutantur testimonia ejus . . .* "

"Santo Padre, you are reading in Latin."

"Ah so? Well, it's beautiful just the same . . . *in toto corde exquirunt eum—*"

Then, with a smile toward Manzù, he shifted into Italian.

"—for they who work iniquity have not walked in his ways."

It was a pleasure to see him like this, reciting Old Testament hymns in Latin as though standing on his toes. Manzù accepted it with relief. Following the death of don Giuseppe, too many nightmares and ghosts had come into his life. Now, before Pope John, they seemed to fall away, like cringing devils before a medieval saint. It was long overdue, for he had taken more than he could handle.

The day after the funeral, he had collapsed. Cardinal Testa, dressed in scarlet, came to see him but Inge sent the prelate away, saying Manzù was too upset to meet anyone. After a few days, the sculptor wrote to Capovilla, saying he felt obliged to dedicate the doors to don Giuseppe; otherwise, he could not go on with them. Capovilla replied by inviting him to come and see the Pope—bringing his tools and clay if he so desired.

Manzù accepted, glad for the chance to do one more study. But above all else, he was anxious to know if they would allow the doors to be dedicated to his friend who was merely a monsignor—a man of many friends, but also of many enemies which was inevitable with such a spirit. A week before dying, for example, don Giuseppe wrote in the Vatican newspaper, *L'Osservatore Romano*, that too many priests behaved like bookkeepers. Besides irritating all bookkeepers in the Holy City, this also irritated all others who felt they had been called to keep accounts for God on the sins of man. Yet here was a priest named Monsignor de Luca, implying there existed sins and virtues which could not be entered onto Christianity's ledger. No, Monsignor. Only a communist could write such nonsense—or worse, a Freemason. "There he goes again," complained Cardinal Testa. "De Luca's always making fun of us cardinals."

So said some. And so Manzù rode to the Apostolic Palace, feeling that the future of his doors for St. Peter's hung in the balance. For without the support of Pope John, he could not dedicate them to his beloved friend. And without that, he would not be able to continue them.

The Pope, however, was not ready to talk about this. He was too deep in the Bible.

"What joy and life there is here!" he exclaimed. "If we

could find a way of getting mankind to sit down and read the Bible as a newly published book, a narrative of man searching for himself, it would become very popular in places where people have forgotten it. Don't you agree?"

"*Sì, Santità.*"

He plunged again into reading the psalms, with a gusto bordering on pure song. It was Good Friday. During the previous day, he had consecrated twelve cardinal deacons as bishops at the Lateran. He had also washed and kissed the feet of thirteen young seminarians. And that morning he had again crossed Rome to celebrate the Good Friday liturgy at St. Paul's—an exhausting ceremony done without ring or mitre or other ornaments of the papal office and, at one point, even without his shoes. On Sunday he would deliver his fourth Easter message to the city and to the world. Meanwhile, he was reading Hebrew hymns, as if they were a source of secret strength for immense labors to come.

After Manzù had set up his equipment, John left the desk to sit in the chair by the window. When this happened, the Pope and the sculptor became immediately aware of their new relationship. In previous encounters, don Giuseppe had stood on the other side of John, next to a large window curtain which was velvet and, with sunshine on it, the color of a lion skin. As Manzù began to work, he found himself looking toward the sunlit curtain. The Pope did the same thing and for a moment Manzù felt himself seized once more by old nightmares and ghosts. Anger and despair bent his spirit, so that he was at a loss for words or the ability to work. Finally, Pope John spoke softly.

"So now we are just two."

"Yes."

He smiled with such warmth and understanding that Manzù knew the Pope felt as he did.

So now we are just two . . .

Without thinking, the sculptor put down his tools and went to stand mutely next to the Pope in the golden chair.

"Tears can change themselves into pearls," said John.

Yes, he thought, if you were an oyster. But he was human and without a shell. He suffered and overflowed from every part. His tears fell to the earth like bitter water and not like pearls.

"I see only my tears."

"The other will come."

"How, *Santità?*"

"You will see it, too. Perhaps on your doors."

That was right, of course. Such a great loss could only be reflected in his work. Don Giuseppe, in his living, had taught him the value of life. In dying, he had confirmed it. Most certainly this would become infused in the bronze panels.

"I'd rather have him alive than anything else."

"Because you loved him, Manzù."

After a moment, he asked: *"Santità,* why did so many love him?"

"He had a special trust in both God and man and it made of his life a very wide human arch. He also had the highest dignity of the priesthood—the spirit of sacrifice, the imitation of Christ. But most of all, there was also this human arch under which so many gathered."

The moment had come to speak of the doors.

"Santità, don Giuseppe helped me so much with the doors that he has now become a part of them. I feel I must dedicate them to him."

"Yes—if you think so, you should do it."

"Grazie, Santo Padre . . . Grazie."

With great relief, he returned to work on the clay. They spoke from time to time, ambling easily from one subject to the next—Bergamo, its new seminary, a visit of the Pope's brothers bringing country ham and bread ("they suspect the soup here is made of angels' hair"), and finally the terrible racket Romans make in their churches ("they should stop shouting—God's not deaf").

When their words faltered, sometimes losing themselves in glances on the curtain's sunlit bank, they would fall into a momentary silence. Then the talk would begin again, easily, as though walking together in the country. Occasionally Capovilla would return to the library, bringing a brief visitor or a message. During those periods Manzù worked rapidly and well, knowing this was going to be the best bust he would do of the Pope.

After an hour and a half, he prepared to leave and John nodded to Capovilla.

"All right," he said, "if you want to bring it in now."

The young secretary left the room briefly, returning with an immense Bible. It was so big he had to carry it in two hands.

"This is for you," said John. "But don't be alarmed—it's not in Latin!"

Capovilla put it on the Pope's desk and for a moment they all looked through it.

"It has another feature," said John. "The words are so big, you can read them without glasses."

He sat down and, taking his desk pen with which he signed memos, bulls and encyclicals, wrote inside the cover of the great book: "To my dear townsman, Giacomo Manzù, an homage of joy and of benediction."

The artist thanked him and, overcome with emotion, left with the big book under his arm. He returned twice again during the next six days and so finished the last bust he was ever to do of John. It sits today in the Vatican Museum and more than any of the others reflects the interior man which he had sought since their first meeting and the ride in the elevator up to the Pope's apartment.

With the last bust completed, the time had come to say goodbye. But John assured Manzù they would see each other soon. Besides the busts and the doors, the sculptor had also agreed to do a new pavement before the entrance of St. Peter's, with a design bearing the papal coat-of-arms and date of Vatican Council II. And he had agreed to make two medallions for the occasion, in October.

"Call me if you need anything."

"*Sì, Santità.*"

"And we'll see each other very soon."

"*Sì, Santità.* Thank you."

"When the doors are finished, we will have a big *festa* and invite everyone."

"*Va bene. Molte grazie.*"

So the sculptor left, filled with pleasure at the thought of the big *festa.* So he left, too, with fresh strength in his heart. John had filled some of the void left by don Giuseppe, emerging as a new island in his life. And that night he thought of him again, standing inside the doorway of the library, saying: "Call me if you need anything."

Only later, upon reading notes in Pope John's private journal, did Manzù discover an entry made four months previous, indicating that also this island was sinking:

"I am aware of the beginning of a certain disturbance in my body that must be natural for an old man. I bear with it calmly, even if it does give me a little annoyance at times and in spite of the fact that it makes me fear it may be growing worse. It is not pleasant to think about it a great deal. But once again, I feel prepared for anything."

Manzù worked hard that summer, especially on the doors, and it was during this period that Cardinal Testa became more difficult. The intrusions finally reached a point where the cardinal sought to change the composition of Death on Earth, by removing the child from the window.

"She should hug her mother's leg, or maybe pull at her dress," he said.

"Why that?"

"To show that she is the daughter and that she needs her mother."

Manzù knew then he needed the Pope. He needed to ask him to remove this man bodily from his studio—if not, they were going to end up badly. Luckily, he had a chance for this in August when he went to see the Pope at Castelgandolfo, to obtain approval of the design for the portico pavement of St. Peter's.

The papal palace at Castelgandolfo is in the Alban hills south of Rome, and Manzù was driven there in a red Triumph sports car by his son, Pio. On the way, the exhaust pipe broke and began to make a terrible racket racing down the highway. Reaching the palace, they went through the main portal and into the old courtyard, with the car sounding like a dive bomber about to crash onto the papal chambers. Attendants and ushers came running to windows and doors, scowling angrily as though awakened from sleep. Manzù was embarrassed at first. Then he recalled how much don Giuseppe would have loved this and felt better.

Pope John was seated in the garden, with a cardinal and a bishop. From a distance, it was an impressive scene. Sunlight slanted in below a ceiling of umbrella pines, bathing everything in a soft and radiant light which seemed to come from the ground itself and so allow the Pope and his guests to appear in distinct outline, each one surrounded by his own special aura of light.

"Look at that," Manzù said, stopping with his son on the gravel path, overwhelmed by the singular beauty of the forms in such a light.

"They're my cardinals," he said.

He had done them a hundred times over, with many robes and different faces, but always in the same basic triangular form. They had gone into museums and exhibitions around the world and millions had seen them. Some critics called them noble and pure—saints with the simplicity of arching arrows, or martyrs mumbling to God. That is what some said. But for Manzù they were only forms. He did not think of the men beneath the robes. Yes, a face, a hand and two feet emerged from the triangle. But inside was a mummy. Let him sleep there. If the vessel spoke to mankind, it was because mankind needed to speak of it, to shout or whisper into the void, into the jug with the outer folds and the two little feet.

Don Giuseppe had loved them. "You have created the ideal form for twentieth century man," he had said one day. "You are not responsible that there is nothing under it, beneath the robes. You have thrown out the challenge of the form. The Church and man must invest it with substance. If your enemies had vision, they would suspect you much more for this than for voting for the Communist, Palmiro Togliatti. But they can't see it, for they are empty, too."

In the garden, the Pope and his visitors stood up as Manzù approached with his son. John wore his plain white cassock, while the cardinal and bishop were in black with colorful capes—a white pillar and bright triangles in the golden light. Yet the difference ran deeper than this. For the cardinal and bishop had form where John had content. Theirs was a promise of substance within the triangle. His was the substance revealed. And to show him in any other way, would be to cloak the naked truth. Manzù had tried, in one of the portraits, to put John in cope and mitre, immersing him within the triangular form of the cardinal. But it did not work, and now he knew why. For with John, the man beneath the robes

198

had already been seen. The promise had been realized. To cover him again would be to cheat. The work still existed in his studio, but he would have to destroy it.

John extended his hand toward the sculptor who in the aura of light saw the smile, the eyes, and felt the touch of the hand as it pulled him toward the waiting cardinal.

"So here he is, my dear friend, the great sculptor Giacomo Manzù, and his son, Pio."

He passed before Cardinal Agagianian and Archbishop Sigismondi. In each he saw reflected the thrust of his words and the touch of his hand as their faces came to life momentarily—then went out again.

John knew why the sculptor had come and, seeing the folder of designs, under his arm, was quick to indicate this was not to be seen by the other visitors. So Manzù said nothing and waited. After a few minutes, Monsignor Capovilla asked the monsignori if they would like to see the other end of the garden. Since it was unthinkable that a papal secretary would separate His Holiness from his guests without previous design, they all agreed quickly with a bobbing of heads and a babble of voices.

Finally alone, John smiled apologetically.

"Even out here, they keep coming," he said.

"It must be difficult, *Santità*."

"Not always. Agagianian is a very learned man. But . . ."

He looked toward their distant figures and sighed.

"In September I will make my retreat, to the new tower in the Vatican garden. I will be alone. I need the silence to review myself—and where I fail."

This surprised Manzù. What sort of tinkering did John do with that mammoth soul? Where did he find his blemishes, his sins? Surely, the interior of a Pope was like the innards of a giant ocean liner: it went on forever. A motor car or a priest might break down, but a liner in mid-ocean or a Pope on the throne—never. Especially John, who was equipped with Catholic theology and fueled from faith which sent him churning ahead—flagship of a global fleet. What repair did he need?

Capovilla returned momentarily to whisper something to John who accepted it with a quiet nod. Quite clearly, his personal tranquility, which the world admired, was not inherited, but rather the product of long spiritual exercises, the fruit of immense labors with himself. All great men—artists, scientists, popes—submerged their personalities into their work. The bigger the ego, the more mammoth the submersion. Yet John's ego, submerged in Christ—how big was it really? It had to be fairly large. Most certainly it was this which he sought to repair in the privacy of his retreat. For Popes, like all men, had to wrestle with their souls . . .

Suddenly Manzù realized Capovilla had left and John was watching him with a smile. He nodded then at the folder, to indicate they could finally discuss it.

"I have the design of your coat-of-arms for St. Peter's portico and some models for the medallions in honor of the Vatican Council."

"Yes? Then let's see them."

Manzù opened the folder on the gravel and the Pope sat down to look at it. The coat-of-arms showed the tower of the Roncalli family which he had selected years ago when first made bishop, and the lion he had placed above the tower upon becoming cardinal of Venice, all of it superimposed upon the crossed keys and tiara of the papacy. Above it was John's name in Latin—JOANNES XXIII PONTIFEX MAXIMUS—and below was the opening date of the

Vatican Council. It had been laid out within a rectangle, rather than the traditional oval form, commonly known as *testa di cavallo*, or horse's head.

"The Vatican engineer wanted it to be a horse-head, but I explained to him that I did not feel like following an ancient theme and proposed we make it a rectangle."

John bent forward, studying the bright work on the stone gravel.

"All right—if you like it rectangular, let's do it that way. Besides, how can you put a lion in a horse-head?"

They laughed and Manzù confided there had been some criticism of his lion.

"They said it is too tame—too much like a kitten."

"Good," said John. "How else is a friendly lion supposed to look? Must he always eat Christians in the Colosseum?"

They looked at the lion, who in turn appeared to stare quizzically back at them, as if waiting for someone to decide about him. Manzù liked him—and so did the Pope.

"He's my type of lion," said John.

"Good," said the sculptor, showing next three studies of medallions for the Council. One represented the Pope in partial profile, with the *camauro* pulled over his ears. John liked that, as he liked the second one showing him seated before a kneeling cardinal. But he rejected the third version, which placed him at the foot of the Cross.

"It's too presumptuous," he said. "I prefer these other two. Will you have all this finished in time for the Council?"

"Yes, *Santità.*"

"We will be ready, too. At first they said we could never prepare for such a council within three years. But we have done it, and with enormous interest everywhere. You can see it out here at Castelgandolfo, in the large audiences. People from every country of the world are confident that the council will be good for the Church. That is very encouraging because we've worked so hard —and for so long."

He paused as Manzù began to close the folder.

"So what do you do now?"

"I must enlarge this design to its actual size, and make patterns for each letter in bronze. Then I must go to Carrara to pick out the marble for its right color, supervise the cutting and see that it is laid into the pavement of the portico."

"All in two months?"

"Sì, Santità."

"Then you should waste no more time talking to an old priest in a garden. How goes my portrait and the doors?"

"Your portrait is fine. Perhaps this last one I did is the best."

"And the doors?"

"I'm afraid, *Santità*, that I am not in accord with the *Signori Cardinali*."

"Eh? That would be Cardinal Testa."

"Yes, Cardinal Testa."

"What's the problem?"

"We have different concepts on art and what should go on the doors."

"But you have not stopped work?"

"No. It goes ahead, but slowly."

"That's not right. Testa is supposed to make sure that you lack nothing."

The Pope shook his head in disapproval.

"In the future," he said, "if you are not in accord with the *Signori Cardinali*, come and see me. But come in the afternoon, because in the morning I'm never free. You can arrange it with the monsignor," he said, meaning Capovilla.

Manzù thanked him and said goodbye, returning with Pio along the garden path. He left with an unexpected sense of sadness, of impending loss, and at the garden's edge, turned to look back. Life was there—lingering on. Above a rising tide of shadows, the last sunlight was a deeper gold. It touched the heads and shoulders of the cardinals, returning now to John, again seated in his lawn chair. Manzù thought of the friendly face smiling in the evening light and then, for a fleeting moment, saw it fading into the night. With a shudder, he turned quickly to continue his walk up the garden path.

In the courtyard they climbed into the red Triumph for a roaring return to Rome. All along the way, Manzù felt the wind and told himself that everything was going well. John had accepted the medallions and the design. He had indicated he would silence the cardinal. And after the pavement was finished, he could begin work on the last three panels of the doors without further interference. Then it would be finished. Thirteen years of heartbreak and nightmare, the stalking ghosts of his life, would vanish. The doors would be up, he would be free, and they would finally have the big *festa* which John had promised.

And also the portrait would be finished. He would send John three or maybe four of the seven plaster busts now in his studio. From these the Pope could choose the one he preferred. Manzù, in the car with the wind in his face, began to think about those he would destroy and, as they passed across his mind, so did the face of John in the fading light of the garden, his lips moving without the sound of the words.

This image was abruptly interrupted as they turned onto the Appia Antica, lined with statues of ancient Romans. They stood near the roadside—forgotten sentinels, wrapped in togas. All of them lacked arms or heads. Yet they seemed to possess more life within their trunks of stone than did the many Romans sprawled about them, seeking life on a Sunday afternoon along the trodden, grassy roadbanks.

From the Appia, they streaked into Rome, over the Tiber river and up the Aventine to Manzù's studio at the Tempio di Diana. He went to work immediately on an enlargement of the portico design and thought no more of his vision of John in the garden. Yet later, upon reading the *Journal*, he found an entry made before their encounter in his luminous garden. Most certainly, this helped explain his strange smile:

"I must think seriously about what is happening to me, that is, about my absolute conformity to the will of God. Perhaps the hour of my gravest difficulty approaches. Just thinking about it upsets me. But as long as I can, I intend to continue that holy detachment which, up till now, has been my best friend . . . "

John's body was being destroyed at its foundations, and he knew it. One month later, an X-ray showed a growth in his stomach which was the same sort of ball that had plunged don Giuseppe into his tomb.

"Don't be disturbed," he told Capovilla. "I am ready, and while there is time left I will do all that the Lord asks of me. Who knows—perhaps these last days of my life, while I still have control of my body, might be the most important."

His doctors confirmed their diagnosis on October 28. Pope John—two hundred sixtieth successor to St. Peter, priest and human being loved by the world—was a terminal case.

"From that moment on," wrote Capovilla in tears, "we saw him go on his *via crucis*, the path of suffering—at first trembling, then unhesitantly, in close union with God."

Yet Manzù was not immediately aware of this. Indeed, from overwork on the pavement design, and the doors which he could not leave alone, he fell seriously ill. It happened, fortunately, after selecting the marble at Carrara. So the pavement was ready for the opening of the Council, although he was unable to witness the event, being under doctor's care in his sister's home in Bergamo.

He recovered to return to Rome in January, when Capovilla phoned to say the Pope had said Mass for his recovery and had remembered him in his prayers. Manzù was touched by both the Pope's and his secretary's solicitude.

"I'm overwhelmed that he should think of me—especially because a Mass is wasted on someone like myself."

"Good," said Capovilla. "You sound like your old self. So I have a request to make."

"Yes?"

"Finish the portrait of the Holy Father. Finish it quickly, please."

There was a note of urgency in his voice.

"What's happened?"

"Nothing. Only they keep pressing for it. You don't need much more time, do you?"

"No, *Monsignore*. I'll have the bronze castings made immediately."

2 - VI - 60
Vaticano

Chapter Sixteen

THERE were seven busts of John in the studio. All of them were in plaster and ready for casting into bronze. Nothing had been done about it, however, because Manzù was not sufficiently satisfied with any of them to make a final choice. Yet now the time had come to do it—to select the best ones, and destroy the others. So he ordered his assistant Mauro to get everything ready for this, and when he came into the studio the next morning, he found a line-up of seven Pope Johns.

It was not a very military line-up. Some stood a bit behind the others, as though humanly incapable of such precision. This was, no doubt, the way Sergeant Roncalli had presented himself for morning roll call with his Italian troops—the big mustache neatly trimmed, but the leggings very sloppy and his brown eyes even more so—wandering out of line and across the faces of other men whose problems and lives were part of his own. They were the ones who, in the early dawn light, clung to shreds of sleep and bits of dreams, withdrawn from the litany of numbers and names. Also withdrawn were some of the busts of Pope John in this studio line-up where a hammer was about to crash onto their faces and so send them into oblivion.

An Artist and the Pope

During the past months, Manzù had thought a great deal about this necessary act of destruction. Yet before beginning it, he looked once more into the seven faces, as one does when saying goodbye to a mixed company of friends and strangers.

Mauro had placed them in their order of development, so that the first one in line was the first bust that had been done. Looking at it now was like staring into the face of an old friend, while Manzù debated with himself on whether or not to destroy it.

—I know you well, and not without bitterness, for you were the first one and the hardest. On you I clung as to a clay cliff when I was fainting. On you I put all that I saw of John from without, seeing humpbacked waves above the battling of whales. You are John the Exterior. I hated you because you were a mask and you hid the real man. Below that half-smile, below the benign face—what is there? Beneath that arching forehead, within that naked dome, what dreams are coiled? What encyclicals still unwritten for the sleeping world? What visions of God have you seen and what more do you want from this shuffling life?

Yet as the sculptor stood there, hammer ready to crush it, he knew that this work, above all others, most perfectly portrayed the Pope as the world best knew him. He could have stopped here, with this first work. He could have laid down his tools at this moment, rather than continue the exhausting race after six more Johns—seeking to find what? The interior of what man? His father, perhaps, without shoemaker nails in his mouth? Or some part of himself which he had given away or lost somewhere?

He did not know. It was too far back up the line and now he could only guess. Man appeared destined to awaken only in the middle of his life. He began his search too far down the road. Meanwhile, there was this work, this sculpture where the road went up the face of a mountain. So let it stand, as it was.

He passed to the next one.

—You're the first one with the *camauro* over the ears and the velvet and ermine shoulder cape. You were a friend to me, for you came more easily than Number One. Your face is deeper, too, with more of the interior man. Yet all of you is better done in Number Three with the same folds in the jowls, the same brow, heavy and low over the face. All of it is better linked together in Number Three. So . . .

He brought the hammer down. It hit, not upon the face, but rather upon the metal armature of the stand. The vibration of the blow cracked the plaster and John's face fell apart, clinging for a moment in two halves as though split asunder by a rough wood ax. It continued to hang that way, like a split white melon, until a second blow sent it all crashing to the floor.

—Number Three, you have all of Two, but not as much as Number Four. Your face is puffy, where Four is strong. I should destroy you as well . . .

He stopped, hammer raised. In his lifetime he had destroyed hundreds of plaster forms and over 150 bronzes. It was a ruthless pursuit, for he wanted no works to endure which caused discomfort. Nothing was lost, or ever could be, if there was the courage to destroy and begin again. As for this one, Number Four, perhaps it would last, perhaps not. It would depend upon how it looked after being cast into bronze. So he passed to the next one.

—Number Five, you are a creature of the studio, born of One and Four, yet not of either. You are not John Exterior, nor are you John Interior. The spirit of John must match the spirit of the sculpture . . .

An Artist and the Pope

He struck the armature, but it would not crack. So he hit this one directly on the forehead and the face crumbled in a shower of plaster. The bone white features—the nose, the ears and large brow, the lips and throat—all of it fell to his feet like a bombed building crumbling and dumping its intimate bedrooms and secret chambers into common rubble upon the street.

The next work was the largest and most imposing of all—a three quarter length of the Pope wearing the cope and mitre as bishop or cardinal. For a long time, Manzù had known this must go. It was too close to the "empty vessel" forms of his cardinal series. The formula had not worked—in fact, it restricted the search for the interior portrait. The stove-pipe vertical of the mitre bore down too strongly upon John's brow. His face seemed crushed beneath it, and his back too bent under the cope. Wanted was the naked man, not an old Pope suffocating with symbols of his office.

—So you go, too, hat and all.

One blow at the mitre took away the top of the head, leaving it open and hollow like an empty flower pot. Second and third blows sent the remaining features onto the floor, leaving a headless cope which was quickly hacked to pieces.

Number Seven was last. This one Manzù had done in three sittings in April and, unlike the others, had never touched it again in the studio—except to place it upon a quarter length body with cape and collar. Of all the busts, this had more of the interior of John. It was also stronger. Where the first one had patience and perhaps love this also showed the wearing effects of those attitudes upon the human body. It also revealed, especially upon the left side of the face, the strength of interior discipline. The right side was softer, suggesting that here the world could more freely enter. And of all the busts, these eyelids were heavier and the lines in the face deeper—as though a tide had withdrawn after a tempest, allowing one to look in wonder at a quiet landscape which had felt the weight of mountains and the drag of oceans. After four years on the throne, the crush of the crown had cut into the man, while the power of his heart drove him on and on. Again Manzù argued within himself.

—You are more the John I know, the man I love, the face that smiles in the garden's evening light. But despite this, you are not perfect. You are not the clear headwaters of the soul which I sought. Still, you will have to do, because I could do no better. I should never have sought to create you, or the others, because I was no longer interested in portraits and could not satisfy your basic demands. It was a mistake to begin you. As a man I made you, and as a man I can be understood. But as a sculptor, no—because as a sculptor I should have said, "I'm sorry, Signor Pope, but I no longer do portraits of anyone since the identity of all human beings intrigues me much more than that of a single one."

He looked back then, along the broken line, at four Johns standing above the white rubble of the fallen three. With gaps in their ranks, the standing four seemed more than ever alone. Each one stared straight ahead at other works in the studio—a naked ballet dancer and, beyond that, two panels for the doors showing death in space and death on earth.

Manzù felt better. The destruction of imperfect works always gave him a sense of relief. What was bad in them was gone. He hoped it was forever, since he would probably never have need to do another portrait of John. So he thought, as he ordered the four busts cast in bronze for presentation to the Pope and eventually to the world.

The bronzes were ready in April and, on the day before

211

Easter, Manzù had them brought to the Apostolic Palace where they were placed on pedestals in the papal library. The Pope's chauffeur and valet helped with this and when everything was ready, Capovilla left the room to get Pope John.

The sculptor waited inside the doorway, where often the Pope had stood to receive him, thinking what a joy this was going to be. Yet when the door opened, and John appeared, he wished it had never happened.

It was another man. The face Manzù had known so well, had molded with his hands and seen in his dreams— the great face like a mountain, was crumbling. Most of it had fallen, except the big hooked nose and the immense ears which were left to ride above all else like alarming sentinals—gaunt towers of a crumbling castle.

He wore a bright mozzetta or shoulder cape, trimmed with white ermine, and on his head was perched a white skullcap. Between the red and white, his flesh seemed yellow. New furrows creased his cheeks, as though ravaged by torrential streams, and under his eyes there lay dark, cavernous hollows.

"Manzù—what have you brought me?"

He smiled in the old way, but his eyes did not rise above the greeting to look into those of his visitor. They came up only halfway, then drifted away. It was this, the failure of the eyes, which was most saddening. The spirit of the man was there, ready and willing to keep his engagement with life. Yet the eyes uncontrollably drifted away, as though aware that nothing could hide that which lay on his face and so caused discomfort to others—the imprint of death. Still, the spirit fought on.

"So many Pope Johns!" he said. "What a harvest of them . . . isn't one of us enough?"

212

Quite obviously, he was delighted with so many and went from one to the other, commenting on each, as though lost in a forest of bronze images.

"Let's see . . . this was the first one, this with the *zucchetto*. Yes, this is where we began."

He passed then to the two busts with the *camauro* over the ears, and immediately became mixed up.

"This came next . . . no, this one. Or is there another one somewhere?"

Puzzled, he looked at Manzù. He wanted the second bust which resembled his mother. Yet it was now a hundred pieces of plaster in the city dump.

"The one you are seeking is incorporated into this one."

John nodded doubtfully, and moved on to the third work.

"So then this was the next, and finally here we are."

He stood now before the last portrait, with the *camauro* and collared cape. The lines were deeper on the face and the Pope, looking at it, nodded to himself. Then he looked back toward the first one. Almost two years separated them in time—while one more year lay between the last figure and the Pope as he appeared at that moment.

"You've done more than give me a portrait," he said. "You've chronicled my pontificate in bronze."

They laughed and once again Manzù noticed the deep hollows under his eyes.

"Which one do you prefer that we keep here?" he asked.

The sculptor put his hand on the last work.

"I prefer this one, not because it is the last or the biggest, but because it satisfies me more than the others."

"I know, I know—you're not content. I know that. So we will keep this one. We will put it in the middle of my office for everyone who comes to see, and I will tell them about you."

This touched Manzù, but he did not know what to say in reply. So they stood in silence and looked at the sculpture.

"It will be here only a little while," said John. "Because as soon as I am dead, they will take it away."

Take it away—where? Manzù was shocked. So the great struggle to cast the man into bronze, the search across three years came down to this brief life—to endure as long as a dying Pope? After that, it would be swept out with the big shoes, the family photographs and the top-heavy tiara. It would be banished by courtiers, lackies and jealous Popes, sent to the Vatican storerooms with the busts of other Popes. Or perhaps it would stand in an empty corner of the Apostolic Palace, unseen except by trembling pilgrims as they waited for the new and living Pope. *Porca miseria*, what a finish.

John proceeded to select the first bust for Capovilla and the third one for San Marco in Venice. That left the one which Manzù liked least. It was the same one he had almost destroyed.

"We could send it to Bergamo," said John.

"If you will allow me, *Santità*, I'm against that. I would not willingly give it to Bergamo. It does not satisfy me. I prefer to destroy it."

John did not agree with this, but did not say so.

"All right—take it if you like. Take it away."

Then he said: "Come and sit down a moment, because I need to sit a while."

They walked to his desk and John sat down weakly.

"Take a seat," he said.

"No, *Santità*, I'll stand."

"And why stand?"

"Excuse me . . . I can't."

"But no," he said. "Do me the pleasure to sit down, otherwise this can go on forever."

So Manzù sat down with him—for the first and last time. He had some color photographs of the portico pavement with the papal coat-of-arms and he showed them to the Pope who was delighted.

"What a splendid lion!" exclaimed John. "And the tower is very good, too."

He sighed and shook his head.

"How kind of you to show these to me. Each time I go in or out of the basilica, they have me up in the air on the portable throne and I can't see anything below me. So I go back and forth over your work and never see it. That's the way a Pope lives. How are the doors coming?"

"I have to finish only three more panels."

"Good—and you like what you've done?"

"I don't know what I've done. I'm so immersed in it. But I think there are some things which do not have to be done again, that can stand alone, that will do."

"And when will it be ready?"

"Perhaps in September."

"Let us know fifteen days ahead of time, so we can have a big *festa*."

Then he said:

"How goes it now with the cardinal?"

It was no better. If anything, it was worse. But Manzù did not want to add further to John's troubles. So he indicated it was all right.

John seemed very pale.

"I'm tired," he said.

Four days earlier, he had signed the greatest encyclical of his reign and perhaps of this century—*Pacem in Terris*. It completed the second half of his other work—*Mater et Magistra*. Together they measured the earth and the heavens and found that nowhere was man a dwarf. Man's dignity was the footstool of the universe and one life was worth all of it. The documents formed a unified field theory of theology.

"After *Pacem in Terris,* you should be able to rest a while."

"Eh, yes . . . yes. But there's so many things still to be done."

"But you've done so much."

"I must review the catechism."

"The catechism?"

The Pope nodded but Manzù still could not believe it. The father of the great encyclicals, the bishop of Rome, the Supreme Pontiff of the Holy Roman Church intended to return to the penny catechism, to the simple instructions of faith, known by heart to every Catholic child. And as if to prove it, he began to recite them in the way children do.

"Why did God make you?" he asked.

Then he replied: "God made me to know Him, to love Him, and to serve Him in this world and to be happy with Him forever in Heaven."

He spoke as though each word was another step down a mountain slope. At the end of his life, he was walking into the valley reciting a child's catechism. The words, as he said them, seemed to explain to him why he had lived as he had, and why he had done certain things.

He knew he loved God, he knew he was the Servant of Servants and that he was ready for death. Yet before going down the hill, he was looking back at what he had done in his life as pastor, diplomat, bishop, and finally the revolutionary Pope who opened the doors of the ancient Church to the modern world. Looking at all of this, he was asking: "Why did I do it?"

So it seemed at that moment—and when he spoke again, there was in his words a reply to this question.

An Artist and the Pope

"St. John Chrysostom tells us—'Remember, my brothers, that one day you will be called upon to give an account, not only of your own lives, but of the life of the whole world.'"

He paused for a moment, as if looking over all the testimony he would have to give.

"So you see, there is still much to be done."

Capovilla approached the desk, anxious to end the session and so spare the Pope any further fatigue. Manzù rose to leave. John also stood up, to embrace him warmly while pretending it was not goodbye—not really.

"As soon as the doors are finished, we will have the *festa*."

"*Sì, Santità.*"

"And if you need anything, I am always here. The afternoons are better, though. Just speak to the *Monsignore.*"

"*Sì, Santità.*"

He had said this before, of course, and it was said again now to show that all was the same as before. The sculptor hurried out before the Pope or his secretary could see the tears in his eyes.

It was a cold April day and the wind blew through the Court of San Damaso. It flicked the cassocks of scurrying monsignori and it slid along the pavement a grey wing feather, fallen from a dove.

How long? wondered Manzù How much longer would John stay with us? How many fallen feathers, how many wind miles remained before he would be asked to testify for himself and the life of the world?

Come ho visto Giovanni morto

Vaticano
3 - VI - 63

Chapter Seventeen

THE answer came six weeks later with a telephone call from Monsignor Capovilla.

"Come," he said. "Come now."

"Did it happen already?"

"It's happening—hurry. And bring your materials for the mask."

"*Subito*," said Manzù, and hung up.

He had expected the call. A few days earlier, Capovilla had phoned to say it was going badly with the Pope. The disease had so weakened him that he could no longer say Mass, and was receiving Communion in bed. These were probably his last days—would the Pope's sculptor also be willing to make his death mask?

The prospect of working on Pope John in such a manner was most unpleasant for Manzù. To bury in plaster a face he had known and loved in life was the reverse of all he had sought during the past three years. The living spirit would be gone. There would remain only the imprint of a dead leaf, the inert flesh. He shuddered. Yet there was nothing else to do, but agree. A death mask was made of all great men—Einstein, Freud, Marx. It was the last embrace of the clinging world. And to make this one of John,

Capovilla needed someone he could trust. So Manzù agreed to do it, although he had never before undertaken such a task.

He knew the basic principles, however, and after receiving the phone call, quickly made ready. Mauro, his assistant, helped prepare a box with the various materials needed—plaster, cord, vaseline, a basin and some cotton. This was loaded into the grey Mercedes and they drove off quickly for the Vatican.

Speeding through the streets, toward the last hours in the life of Pope John, Capovilla's anguished voice stayed with the sculptor: "Hurry, hurry"—as though they were already beating on the door, to remove the body and make ready for the next Pope.

"Go faster, Mauro. Go through even the red lights."

"I've gone through two already."

Later Manzù was to learn in what manner Capovilla's desperate call was conditioned by the final episodes in John's life, leading to the last scene where the sculptor was to play his role. These events also explain much of what he saw and felt when he reached the Vatican. For each death spins itself out within a measured framework of time, so that the dignity and drama of the last moment depends greatly upon those leading up to it.

John, who had noted the growth of the disease within his body, sensed that it was going to burst its confines and seize him precisely when he began the greatest event of his reign—the Vatican Council. A few days after the meeting with Manzù at Castelgandolfo, he had said: "I know what my personal role will be at the Council—it will be one of suffering!"

He was right. Two weeks after the Council began, on October 28, 1962, his doctors confirmed he had cancer of the stomach and one month later—on the night of November 26—he suffered his first serious hemorrhage. His doctors were alarmed, and his secretary in tears.

"Stay calm," he said. "I'm ready to go when called by the Lord. But that has not yet happened. I'm not dead yet and there's much to be done."

The bleeding stopped, after large plasma infusions, and his recovery seemed miraculous. Audiences, suspended for 15 days, were begun again. He appeared to be past all danger. Yet John knew better. Constant stomach discomfort reminded him that his days were counted. He accepted it with calm and continued working, meeting bishops of the great Council, audiences of pilgrims, and visiting prelates. He left the Vatican to visit churches, institutions and personal friends. He canonized saints and delivered a flood of speeches, letters, radio messages—as well as the last, great encyclical, *Pacem in Terris*, or Peace on Earth.

During all of this, he carried with him the rooted and burgeoning ball that was to drag him to his death. Yet he bore it with cool realism, saying: "I know I will go as did Radini"—his beloved bishop who had died in his arms. So death became a partner in his life and he accustomed himself to it. He had been preparing for it since his seminary days, when he was a youth of 21, and the quitting of life could only be conceived in terms of what he had done with his interior self.

"Even if I were to be Pope," he wrote in his diary, "even if my name were to be invoked and revered by all and inscribed on marble monuments, I should still have to stand before the Divine Judge, and what would I be worth then? Not much."

Now he was 82 and still holding up a lantern to better judge himself. There was no time to rest on a set of propositions about God, because faith was not a resting place. Faith was always being found along the way—increasingly solid and satisfying as one received evidence of transcendence in conscious experience. Yet because God was infinite and utterly transcendent, He could never be fully reached. There was, instead, an ascent toward God—made through man's individual and cultural growth in self-consciousness. This was the heart of John's pastoral revolution, manifest in his person and then in Council documents. It drove him on and on, even in his last days.

So he went down like a great ship, with all flags flying, the motors pumping and the quarter-deck awash, yet holding the vessel on its true course until it finally sank beneath the waves.

Montecassino was one such bearing. John had promised to visit the rebuilt abbey on its hillside above the sea near Naples. As the date drew near—May 23—he told his secretary of state that he intended to keep his word. He had difficulty walking, but that did not matter. He was going anyway. His doctors then heard about it, and said it was too dangerous. The Pope could die on the road. He had to be stopped.

The task of doing this fell to Capovilla—one of many times during John's last days when the great weight of the sinking Pope was shifted onto the shoulders of the frail young priest. Capovilla tackled it by pretending to be humiliated at having to learn about the decision from the secretary of state, rather than from the Pope himself.

"Is it true?" he asked.

"Yes, but don't speak so loudly."

John glanced toward a nearby doctor, then lowered his voice.

"Let's not tell him about it."

"You see? That's one of my reasons. *Santità*, will you allow me five minutes to explain this business?"

"Eh! If I don't give them to you, you'll take them anyway."

Capovilla quickly explained three reasons against the trip—it was a danger to his life, the Italian government was in crisis, and the Benedictine monks, who ran the Montecassino abbey, had failed to keep an earlier promise to the Pope, thus he had no obligation to them.

"Listen, we agree in part. But, as I told you before, the first argument doesn't work."

"Why not, *Santo Padre*? I'm speaking frankly. You could have an hemorrhage."

"I'd go to bed. I'd go into a cell of the monastery. Think of it. To die at Montecassino—the great abbey, the cradle of monasticism!"

"No, *Santo Padre*, don't say such things, don't say them!"

"*Beh*, let's look at the second agrument. The second one holds up better. The third one doesn't, though, because the Pope can't bargain with monks—it's not in good taste. But the government crisis is worth considering, especially after *Pacem in Terris*. Some newspapers might say the Pope is making the trip to help some political party . . . "

Capovilla quickly agreed.

"Fine . . . so you can phone this right away to Cardinal Cicognani."

"Oh, you can tell him. There's no need for any ceremony about it."

"No, no, *Santo Padre*, you tell him because you gave the first orders."

John did not make the trip, and one week later the worst fears of his doctors became an awful reality: the poisonous ball of death broke loose, entering his stomach wall and causing peritonitis. It inflamed tissues, and it seared him with pain. In his bed, he took it without sobbing or crying out. Like a great bull with a mortal wound, he clamped shut his jaws and waited for what came next. Then, as the doctors prepared to give him the first heavy sedation, he opened his soft brown eyes and said: "I want nothing more than to follow the will of God."

He was now locked in with what he described as his "sister death." From that moment on, they would go it together, step by step, to the final pass. And he did it as gracefully as possible.

There was, first of all, the transference of command. For this, he accepted his dark sister upon the quarter-deck of his life with all the dignity and style of a great admiral taking leave of his fleet. The brief ceremony took place as once again it fell to Capovilla to bear the burden, to carry the news that his Pope was about to die. Entering the bedroom, he found John awake in bed, rosary in hand, contemplating the large ivory crucifix on the opposite wall. Capovilla, desperately seeking to control himself, knelt at the bedside and kissed John's hand.

"How do you feel?" he asked.

"I feel all right now. I'm calm. I'm here with the Lord. But I'm also a bit worried.

"*Santo Padre*, it's not you who should be worried—it's me and the doctors. I've spoken to the doctors."

"So what do they say?"

"*Santo Padre*, I'll be loyal to you, as you were with Monsignor Radini. I'll tell you that this is the *dies Domini*, the *dies Christu Iesu*. This is the day you are called into Paradise!"

Capovilla burst into tears on his knees and buried his face in the bed covers. He felt the hand of the Pope tenderly stroke his head and in between sobs he heard John's gentle reproach:

"Look at that, look at that will you—my secretary, who seems so strong and hard-headed, all broken up as he tells his superior the most beautiful thing anyone can tell a priest: 'Today you will go to Paradise.' "

Capovilla continued to sob.

"Oh, don Loris . . . did you hear me?"

"*Sì . . . sì, Santo Padre.*"

"So come now, get up. You know the ceremony of a bishop. I'm a bishop and I must die as a bishop, with simplicity, yet with majesty. Everything must be done right. Go and advise everyone—Cardinal Cicognani, don Angelo dell'Aqua, don Battista, and my family. Also bring the Viaticum. You come, too, with the boys and the confessor. But do everything with great dignity."

Capovilla continued to sob, as though this was the last moment he would ever have with his Pope.

"Come, come, my son. You must be courageous. You have to arrange everything. So begin to get the people together."

"*Santo Padre*, I've already done it. They are waiting outside the door."

John smiled.

"What a rascal! He does everything and doesn't tell me about it. All right, send in the confessor."

Capovilla turned to go, but John called after him.

"No, first the Secretary of State—for his last audience."

Cardinal Cicognani, who loved John as a friend before he became Pope, was waiting impatiently outside the room.

"So?" he asked.

"Go on in," said Capovilla, opening the door. "Go in—it's a day to rejoice!"

He almost screamed it, and the startled cardinal scudded

225

past into the bedroom. John greeted his friend with the 121st Psalm, in Latin:

"*Laetus sum in his quae dicta sunt mihi,*" he began. "I was glad when they said unto me, Let us go into the house of the Lord."

Cicognani also knelt at the bedside, kissing the papal ring. But John quickly indicated he wanted to keep this last meeting within the pattern of their regular morning encounters.

"Do we have something urgent to finish off?" he asked, withdrawing his hand from Cicognani.

The question was a frank admission that their friendship and John's papacy was about to end. It caused the old cardinal to sob on his knees. Tears ran down his cheeks as he shook his head and said just the opposite of what he really felt.

"No, *Santità*, everything goes well."

"Tell me everything," said John. "As long as I'm alive, you should tell me everything. I count on you to handle all the business—but be sure to tell me if you need anything."

Blinking through his tears, Cicognani shook his head.

"Are you sure?" asked John. "You're not holding something back . . . about the Council, maybe?

"No, no."

Cicognani said they were receiving messages and telegrams from all over the world. Kings and queens and prime ministers were praying for Pope John. So was President Kennedy. And men and women of other faiths were praying, too.

"So much, so many people," replied John. "What does it mean, if not that we are all one before the Lord? *Ut unum sint.*"

He repeated the words originally spoken by Jesus after the Last Supper: "That they may be one."

"We are all praying," said Cicognani, "for a miracle."

John did not expect anything of the kind. His last hour had come and he knew it.

"You're sure there is nothing left for me to sign?" he asked again.

His confessor, Bishop Alfred Cavagna, entered next. They met with the sobriety of two old hunters. This was the moment they had explored in theory over thousands of hours—during weekly confessions and in the longer retreats each year, when John withdrew from the Vatican to Castelgandolfo or to his hideaway tower in the gardens. Alone together, the Pope and his "spiritual adviser" had explored the great plain of Christian asceticism—finding its primary seeds in the ideal of true poverty, as first formed by Judaism, in the Psalms, and then in the beatitudes of Matthew and especially those of Luke. They had done this with the eyes of eagles, the introspection of lovers, the absorption of children seeking seashells, and the wonder of men finding new stars. It was what John called his "good road"— and now he was at its end, with his fellow seeker by his side to accept his last words, his doubts, and his faith. John began it with the formality of ancient ritual.

"Bless me, Father, for I have sinned."

He then recounted those places in his life and mind where he believed himself to have sinned by omission, or by failure of act. After he had done this, his bishop-confessor gave him his penance: to offer up his sufferings for the glory of the Church, for the success of the Vatican Council, for Christian unity, and for humanity's search for peace on earth.

"God, I'm sorry for all my sins," said John, as Cavagna gave him absolution, then administered Holy Communion. A communion prayer followed and during this, the door was opened to allow into the room Cardinal Cicognani,

An Artist and the Pope

Monsignori Angelo dell'Acqua and Antonio Samore from the Secretariat of State, as well as Capovilla and the Pope's nephew, Monsignor Giambattista Roncalli. The five nuns who served the Pope came in, too, but stayed near the doors, while everyone else gathered on their knees around the bed.

The Pope's sacristan, Archbishop Peter Canisius van Lierde, entered next with holy oils to give the last rites. He annointed all those parts of the body which might have led John into sin: eyes, ears, nose mouth, hands—and feet. All that remained now was the prayer of the *proficiscor*, commending his departing soul to God.

But John was not ready—for suddenly he sat upright in bed.

"That's enough for now," he said. "I want to talk to you all."

The little group, praying on their knees around the bedside, looked up in surprise. The Pope wore a simple white shirt with short sleeves and sitting up in bed seemed as lively as a saint in a Renaissance fresco—busy talking with God while everyone else had collapsed into a mumble of prayer.

John, however, wanted to talk to those gathered around him.

"*Basta*," he said again, meaning he had had enough ritual.

"Do you know why I keep that crucifix on the wall opposite my bed and not on the ceiling or some place else?"

The little group blinked at the crucifix and waited for the answer.

"It's there so that I can see it with the first glimpse in the morning, and the last one at night. It is there, too, so that I can talk to it during the long evening hours. Look at it, see it as I do. Those open arms have been the program

228

of my pontificate, a modest and humble one, if you will, but I'm satisfied with what I've done and how I've done it and I ask the Lord's grace that my program may continue. Those open arms say to me that they are the Church because Christ died for all men—no one excepted. We have no other program and cannot have any other than the Cross and charity which descends from it."

Then he spoke to each person present, beginning with Cardinal Cicognani.

"Take my words to all the cardinals," he said. "And to the missions and the dioceses of the world. Bear witness, I beg of you, for them all. First of all, about the council— what a heavenly inspiration!"

He repeated the phrase—"heavenly inspiration"—twice more, then continued.

"It will be a great event for the Church. Tell them that and may all my cardinals be united with the bishops in the three aims of the council: to renew us from within, to bring our separated brethren into one Church, and to show to the whole world, all mankind, that we are one family."

He paused, then to Monsignor dell'Acqua he commended his dictum for unity, as though it alone could prevent St. Peter's bark from eventual shipwreck. "*Ut unum sint*, don Angelo. Never forget it—*ut unum sint.*"

For each of the others, he had some words.

To his nephew, he said: "*Caro don Battista*, remember to say hello to everyone for me—embrace them. And you—never forget that as a priest you should live with extreme simplicity."

Of Capovilla, he asked to be forgiven for all the trouble he had caused him: "I hope that I have never been a bad example for you."

To his physician, Piero Mazzoni, he said: "When I kneel

to pray, I thank the Lord for having sent me such a kind and wonderful doctor."

So it went, as he passed from one to the other—touching all in such particular ways that each one seemed to be left before a mirror of himself. He spoke, too, of the Rome diocese, of the Curia, of Bergamo, and Bulgaria and Turkey and Greece. He recalled his time in France and his love of Venice—coming, finally, to his family and the people of his village of Sotto il Monte.

"I beg to be forgiven by all those whom I might have offended in my life, for I have loved them all."

It lasted almost an hour and it caused many to weep, while others dried their tears as though taking strength from the wisdom of a patriarch. John's voice was calm and clear throughout and when it was over, he lay back in his bed and smiled as though he was ready for whatever came next.

Slowly everyone withdrew, except Capovilla, who remained by the bedside.

"So I'm not yet dying?"

"Not yet, *Santo Padre*."

"It's not the moment?"

"Not the moment."

"Will I suffer much?"

"No, no, *Santo Padre*."

"You know, I'm not acquainted with these things. So you must tell me. Make sure to do all that's possible while I am all right. Right now I can think quite clearly. And I can speak well—really well. I have some strength, too, because I feel it. So I don't know if I must die today or not."

"*Santo Padre*, it's like that. We are in the hands of the Lord. Today, tomorrow—as He wants it."

"So how will it happen?"

"You will lose your strength, little by little. You will

not be able to speak. But we will be next to you, in prayer."

"You will not leave me?"

"No—we will never leave you."

"I'm sorry to detain around my person so many people, so many good people."

During the day, visitors came to see him and often their tears touched his hand before their lips could do so. John sought to be as cheerful as possible.

"*Coraggio*," he said. "Courage—it's not yet the hour of the requiem, as you can plainly see."

Capovilla remained as much as possible by his side and, from time to time, John spoke his isolated thoughts.

"I fear, I fear for my dear children, I fear they may be engulfed in another war."

Later, he touched the pectoral cross which lay on his bedstand. It was a simple one which he had bought 36 years ago in a Milan second-hand store.

"Bury me with this only," he said.

The day passed in this manner and, as it drew to a close, the pain overwhelmed him. At first he bore up, swimming through it with broad strokes of prayer. Each engulfment, however, left its imprint. His face, at times contorted in agony, began to slowly broaden and open up, as though lit by an internal light. The pain increased and he sought to accept it with grace and resignation. But it was not easy. In between sedations and in moments of lucidity, he spoke of the great men in his life. He recalled Radini and *Papa* Sarto—Saint Pius X—who had touched his head with words of love, and who had also died in this same room. At other times, when he was alone or not speaking, his eyes drifted slowly over the photographs on the wall, coming to rest finally upon the great ivory crucifix.

"*Ut unum sint*," he said, softly, over and over.

As the night came on, his words became less and less distinct. When his three brothers and sister arrived, together with Cardinal Montini, he was under sedatives. Also present was his niece, Sister Anna, who had flown from her convent in Asmara. They sat and stood about in the shuttered room, waiting for the end. But it did not come immediately and at midnight, while Capovilla was celebrating Mass in the adjacent chapel, John suddenly awakened. To the amazement of everyone, he sat up and recognized his assembled family, speaking to each one by name—Giuseppe, Alfredo, Zaverio, Assunta, and Sister Anna.

"You shouldn't look so sad," he said. "Jesus said 'I am the resurrection and the life.' You know what that means. It is very clear to us all. Physical death is the beginning of the true life."

To the delight of everyone, he asked for some coffee and milk. It was refused him, but a ray of hope ran through those present. Maybe he would live. Maybe this was a miracle. His doctors knew better, however, and soon the pain returned, growing in intensity until he had to have more medication and sank once again into a coma. Cardinals came and went. The Bishop of Bergamo came, too, at a moment when John was lucid. He asked that his diocese be blessed and John replied: "With all my heart."

His strength began to leave him and John felt it going, saying: "I have been able to follow my death step by step, and now I am moving gently toward the end."

To help his breathing, the doctors gave him an oxygen mask, and said: "His life is now at its end—like a candle."

At that moment Capovilla had called for Manzù to come and make the death mask. And now, in the twilight race across Rome, the sculptor saw evidence that John was dying. People stood before newsstands, reading the headlines: "Giovanni Dying" and "Pope Slowly Fading." The

232

latest medical bulletins came over the car radio: "Physicians of the Holy Father announce that death is now approaching. The Pope has begun to retrace the footsteps of Christ up the hill to Calvary." The Vatican Radio's call sign, *Christus Vincit*, began to chime over and over—until Manzù shut the radio off.

"Go faster, Mauro," he said again, causing the Mercedes to hit 100 kilometers an hour down the Lungotevere dei Tebaldi.

From a distance, they saw first the giant television search lights, playing on the brown walls of the old palace, probing against closed shutters for the figure of the man who lay within, dying in an old oak bed. Then they saw St. Peter's Square, packed with people and resembling a vast amphitheater. Upon coming closer, police stopped the car and there was a maddening delay while Manzù explained his mission to an unbelieving cop—finally being allowed to inch through the crowd toward the distant Arch of the Bell.

It was like plunging underwater. In a half light, kneeling and standing, figures appeared as still as waiting fish. They lay under a many-fathomed silence, broken only by a running murmur of prayer, mixed with the sound of the Vatican Radio coming over thousands of transistors: "The Pope is in a coma and slowly fading—nothing more can be done, but pray." The chimes of *Christus Vincit* emerged from radios held next to ears, under arms, inside pockets and beneath buttocks where they served as seats. There were so many that the sound seemed to come from the people themselves—thousands of men and women hooked onto one sound wave, one heart beat and one murmuring prayer as they looked up at the little window and waited for the man they respected and loved to be finally released from this life.

The piazza had become a church without a rooftop.

Its altar was behind the wooden shutters, a plain bed where the dying Pope had said: "This bed is an altar! An altar calls for a victim. Here, I am ready. I have before me a clear vision of my soul, of my priesthood, of the Council, of the universal Church . . . I am at peace. My desire has been always to do the will of God, always, always. I pray for the Church, for children, for priests and bishops that they may be holy, for the whole world . . . ."

Chapter Eighteen

Once through the Arch of
the Bell, Manzù's car sped around the rear of the great
basilica, tunneling through small courtyards until it reached
the San Damaso courtyard. Mauro slammed on the brakes
and the two men started to jump out, but a gendarme insisted that they park the car to conform with the line-up of
others in the courtyard. After this, they took the elevator
up to the top loggia and into the papal apartment.

They waited first in the attendance room with the flag
of Venice and its golden lion. Manzù remembered how John
had admired it, that first day—saying only *"beata Venezia"*
—and suddenly felt a fresh wave of sadness. So it was *addio*
to this, too. John would never make it now. *Pappa* Sarto
had done it, but only after he had been dead for forty years
and declared a saint. They renamed him Saint Pius X, put
silver gloves on his hands, a silver mask over his face, then
placed him in a glass coffin and hauled him up to Venice
and back to Rome by horse, train and boat. John most certainly never intended to travel like that. His *beata Venezia*
meant going there alive, with a sniff of the sea, the cry of
the gondoliers, and the ring of church bells in the mist . . .

Capovilla appeared suddenly—pale, haggard and more
gaunt than ever.

"Come," he said.

They followed him into a smaller waiting room where there were two monsignori reading their breviary, and a bishop holding onto his pectoral cross. After a moment, the bishop was summoned and left. The monsignori were called next and they closed their books and moved out. Manzù and Mauro waited alone. Two baskets, with materials for the mask, sat on the floor next to them. In a distant room a phone began to ring, but no one picked it up and finally it stopped. Beyond this, a voice urgently called for someone named Mario, saying "bring two of them, no, three . . .", followed by a door being closed. Two nuns came into the room, but upon seeing Manzù and his driver, turned around and walked out. Finally, Capovilla returned.

"Come with me now," he said.

Both stood up, Mauro holding the mask materials. Capovilla indicated, however, that he wanted to see Manzù alone. In the corridor, he explained John had not yet died. If Manzù desired, he could pay his last respects to the Pope. The sculptor said he did and Capovilla took him by the hand.

"It can happen any moment—come."

The bedroom was in semi-darkness. A bed lamp, turned toward the wall, cast a low light on John who lay on his back under an oxygen mask. He was wheezing heavily, his big chest alternately gasping upward for air, then collapsing into a still, silent moment which each time seemed to be the last. His face, under the light, was yellow and swollen from sedatives and suffering. Over it lay a white beard stubble.

—*Porca miseria!* Where was death? Why didn't it come and remove him from this terrible agony? Death was the only answer, but death was a dirty whore. She came when you didn't want her and when you did, she was around the corner grabbing someone else who never asked for it. That was death for you—thief, whore and cheat. It was proof that God did not exist—or that He was not a merciful God. For how could he so torment the great heart of

238

man, so reduce him to this pitiful state? Mercy was not with-held by those who knew love. So where was God's great love? It was outside the ballgame, that's where, with death's work better done by man himself.

He knelt then to say goodbye, to make the last touch of flesh to flesh, of man to man, of life to life, thinking:

—This is it, the final vision of John's self plus more, of him plus me plus you plus thee plus all thine and mine too, plus all of us and all of mankind who are truly, verily, really the men of goodwill. The man full of light. The rock. Hail rock. The bending brow of the cliff, the bending . . .

The hand was boiling hot and Manzù withdrew his lips, wondering how John could remain alive and carry such heat through his veins. How was it that his blood did not bubble within its arteries? Incredible. He touched the hand with his own, to make certain his lips had not lied. It was like a wood stove.

—Madonna . . .

Slowly Manzù's eyes adjusted to the darkness and, looking across the bed, he saw a number of people sitting in chairs and staring at him. They were, for the most part, John's family—the three brothers and the sister Assunta. There was also the niece who was a nun, Sister Anna from Asmara, counting her rosary beads.

Manzù recalled his own family sitting in the room where his mother, and then his father, had died—both in an oak bed similar to this one of John, which his sisters now used in Bergamo. A mother's death could be a terrible uproot-ing and a father's could be the crashing of a giant fir tree. But he did not experience at the death of his parents what he felt now with John. Perhaps, as a youth, he had been too exhausted from work to feel much of anything when his parents died. Or perhaps it was because sculpture at that moment had become his real life and was the only love that could claim him.

Yet he had not kissed the hand of his mother or of his father as he kissed John's, or as he kissed the cheek of don Giuseppe. Quite clearly, his true parents had not died in Bergamo, but rather in Rome. They had been a priest and a Pope.

Upon rising he found Capovilla by his side. They withdrew then into the corridor where the secretary explained that the doctors now were saying they did not know when John would die. It might occur within a few hours, or perhaps not happen until the next day.

"So you'd better go home and I will call you . . . when it happens."

"*Va bene.*"

Manzù wanted to tell Capovilla how sad he felt for him, too, and how he also felt a terrible loss. But he said nothing and they shook hands with unexpected formality. The enormous intimacy of John's dying engulfed everything, causing all other acts of the living to appear as mechanical and meaningless gestures made by puppets.

"So I'll wait for your call."

"*Sì, sì,*" said Capovilla turning to meet two pasty-faced monks pulling at his sleeve, one holding a glass jar containing a petrified relic of a finger of a saint.

John lived on, incredibly, through the next day and into Monday. In his last hours he murmured the names of the saints he had canonized and those he held close to his heart—Saints Joseph, Mark, Carlo Borromeo, Gregorio Barbarigo, Pius X.

At one point, his nephew Zaverio unwittingly stood at the foot of the bed, blocking the dying Pope's view of the large ivory crucifix on the wall. John frowned, but no one seemed to get the message. Finally, he lifted his hand and managed to blurt out to the startled group: "Get out of the way!" This sent everyone scurrying as though John was at that moment leaving this earth for his heavenly trip.

Soon after that, he lost the ability to speak clearly, though his eyes indicated he understood all that was happening. He held his old pectoral cross in his hands and when Cavagna gently brought it to his lips, John was able to murmur: *"Dominus meus et Deus meus."* He also said *"Cupio dissolvi et esse cum Christo."* The Pope's confessor then began to read the Mass. But when he saw John's eyes watching him, it became too much for the old man's heart and he had to be relieved.

John's fever rose to 103 degrees early Monday and, with the words *"Mater mea, fiducia mea,"* he drifted into a deep coma. By noon his temperature had reached 105.8 degrees and Professor Pietro Valdoni said: "The Pope is in the hands of God. Clinically he is already dead."

Toward twilight the fever dropped suddenly—sign that his body had now given up the battle and was ready for the entry of sister death. That evening, Mass was said before St. Peter's by Cardinal Traglia. Over 80,000 people filled the piazza, but during the service they were so silent that the splash of the fountains could be heard with the words of the liturgy. Upstairs, in the papal apartment, John's family and his attendants had gathered around a television set, to better follow the Mass from a room adjacent to where the Pope lay dying. From his post near the door, Professor Antonio Gasparrini heard the rhythmic, labored breathing of his patient suddenly catch—and go silent. Quickly he returned to the bedroom. John, attended by thousands in the square and millions of others around the world, had died the way most men do—alone.

The doctor pressed his ear against the Pope's chest. Then, to those hastily gathered around the bedside, he said: "He has expired." Capovilla turned on the room's bright lights and the old doctor, still at John's side, burst into tears.

In the square below, an evening breeze tossed the altar candles as Cardinal Traglia murmured: *"Ite, Missa est"* — Go, the Mass is over. It was 7:49 P.M .

Manzù was called immediately by Guido Gusso, the Pope's valet. With Mauro and another assistant, he once again raced through the city, fighting his way past the police and edging slowly through the packed piazza, reaching the apartment within 35 minutes.

Capovilla met them — a shocking sight. His face was dark with beard stubble and fatigue. Sleepless nights had reduced him to moving with the slow, sodden reflex of a man underwater. His mind, having seen too much, now seemed turned inward, away from reality. There was no contact in his deep brown eyes. They touched in a glance, then drifted away in the manner of a child, lost in a crowd, who no longer believes that strangers can comprehend such words as "home" or "mother" or the name of a favorite doll.

At first Capovilla even failed to realize why the sculptor had been summoned.

"And now?" he asked, apparently referring to the tragedy of the broken pontificate.

"Terrible," replied Manzù.

"I have no words left," he said.

He looked at the floor, as though a great hole had suddenly yawned up before them. Manzù waited a moment, then decided it would help to remind him of their mission.

"We're ready," he said.

"For what?"

"To do . . . as you asked."

Mauro and the second assistant held the materials of their macabre mission — vaseline, plaster, cotton, a tin basin and tough thread — in open baskets. Capovilla, seeing all this, nodded he understood and was finally ready to admit that the man he most loved was ready to receive a mask of plaster which would shut the eyes and nose and mouth in the final, immutable imprint of death.

"*Sì, sì,*" he said with his own eyes closed, turning down the corridor.

Manzù followed numbly with his aides. When they came upon a nun who was weeping, the sculptor turned away from further sight of her sadness, knowing he was near the breaking point himself and could not take much more.

The bedroom he had last seen in semi-darkness, was now brightly lit and John lay in his bed like one who was waiting for someone to speak to him. The sly tricks which the living play upon the dead had not yet begun. His hands, swollen from injections, remained naturally by his side—not yet folded together over his paunch to better clasp a cold metal crucifix. His mouth was slightly open, as though still murmuring "*Mater mea, fiducia mea*"—or even shouting at his nephew to get out of the way so that he could die while looking at the ivory crucifix. They had closed his eyes so that he seemed to be waiting only for a gentle word or a friendly nudge.

What was difficult to witness were the others—infinite variations of the wasted Capovilla. John's brothers stood in a corner with the motionless hulk of unharnessed plough horses. Two doctors, bent like exhausted oarsmen, sat in a far corner, one speaking in a low voice while the other filled out a prepared form. Next to them, reading a prayer book and heedless of anything around her, was John's sister, Assunta. Sister Anna, the nun, sat weeping in another chair.

Manzù stood in a distant corner, waiting for the room to empty and so begin his work. But no one left. After a moment, the nun got up and, taking a pair of scissors from her pocket, cut off some of John's hair.

This, he thought, was going to be the hour of the pirates.

They would soon start lifting the Pope's shoes, his clothes and whatever else could be carried away in snips and snatches. But little happened. The nun wrapped the hair in a piece of paper, buried it in the folds of her dress, and sat down and began to count her prayer beads. A few priests and monks came to stare at John and whisper to one another, then hurry out. Capovilla entered with a white-bearded Cardinal and spoke to John's sister Assunta, reading her prayer book.

"Look," he said. "It's Cardinal Tisserant."

He said it with the air of someone announcing a doctor who had arrived in time to work a miracle. But the aged cardinal quite clearly thought otherwise. He had a scraggly white beard, topped by a red face which seemed choked with suppressed rage. His eyes were blue and cold and he looked around the room as though everyone in it was responsible for the death of John.

"The Cardinal Tisserant," said Capovilla, this time with less certainty.

"*Buona sera*," said the Pope's sister, looking up at the cardinal, then returning to her reading with the grace of a duchess dismissing a gardener. Tisserant seemed even more angry at this and, after a glance at the Pope, quickly left.

Shortly thereafter, he returned with two other cardinals and a little gold hammer. They stood around the bed and began to hit John on the forehead with the hammer, calling him by his name: "Roncalli—are you alive or dead?"

When there was no response from the bed, they hit John again with the hammer and repeated their question: "*Roncalli, Angelo—sei vivo o morto?*"

The performance of the ancient ritual—to determine whether the Pope was truly dead and incapable of answering his family name—had no dignity or reason for Manzù. Nor did the question itself make sense. If he was dead, how could he be expected to answer? If he was alive, or if there was even a chance of it, why hit him on the head?

They did it again, asking the same stupid question with the hammer thudding once more on that deep and noble forehead Manzù knew so well. Unable to any longer control himself the sculptor turned to the seated doctors.

"*Porca miseria!* You're here, can't they ask you if he's dead or not?"

From their corner, the two doctors nodded soberly in agreement.

"So why hit him on the head?"

But it was useless. The cardinals had gone, taking all answers with them. Soon others began to leave. The doctors went first, followed by John's three brothers and sister. Capovilla came and finally went, leaving Manzù alone to begin his grisly job. As his assistants mixed the plaster, the sculptor approached the bed with an acute and unbearable sense of melancholy.

Here was a man, he thought, and look at him now. Regardless of his importance, big or little, he was a real man. That was something in itself, because there were not many of them.

It was the face which impressed Manzù more than anything else, more than the outpressing figure in the white nightshirt, so terribly still in the tiny bed—more than even death itself which he had learned to look upon in childhood, during the influenza epidemic when he helped put them, the naked dead, in lime-soaked shrouds within identical wooden boxes, bearing them finally to the cemetery behind a raised crucifix like the disastrous return of a lost crusade.

Here was one of the world's great sovereigns. Yet now he lay alone and deserted with the face of a *povero uomo*, a plain man. Death gives to each one his face and, looking now at John's, Manzù hoped that he would have a face like that—of a simple man. Then he noticed the hand, swollen and punctured from injections, and thought that this, too, was part of John's portrait. For this was the hand that had signed *Pacem in Terris*.

They began then to make the mask, covering first the face with a coating of vaseline. Next, a nylon cord was placed to run down the brow, along the ridge of the nose and across the middle of the mouth—dividing the face in half. This was to be pulled up, before the plaster became hard, so that the two halves could be lifted free of entrapping crevices without risking damage to the face itself. The nasal orifice was closed off with cotton, the chin held up to block the oral cavity, and plaster was applied until it covered the face, round and smooth as a white melon.

Manzù supervised this with a growing sense of sadness. However noble the purpose, the action itself was undignified and so contrary to his sensibilities that he had trouble breathing. Finally, with John's face entombed beneath the hardening plaster, it was as though they had bottled up the man himself, imprisoning any shreds of the soul which might possibly have lingered behind.

"Let's do the hand," suggested Manzù. "The right one which signed *Pacem in Terris*."

This was less displeasing, and seemed just as important as the mask. After this, it was necessary to wait for the plaster to harden on the still-warm flesh. Manzù waited by the window, where he looked through the shutters at the crowd massed in the piazza.

They were still there, thousands of them, forming a massive block of silence and upturning wonder. He looked down upon them, as they looked up toward him, and knew this was a moment of history which he should try to recognize and understand in the instant of its happening, at the moment of its birth, rather than later when others who had not been there would seek to give their own version of what had happened.

It seemed to him at that moment that once or twice

in a generation a dying monarch or a dead hero is picked to represent the dignity and continuity of a nation's life. This was happening now—not just in this ancient cobble-stone oval, but far beyond it—in other piazzas and homes and chapels around the world, where millions of people had followed this death, step by step. Their mumbled prayers, their muted stares were more than strangled good-byes. They were a massive vote, an act of belief that divisional hatred was not the only reality of the human condition.

There was something else in all men—however prone to evil. It was a capacity for goodness, an empty chamber which could be reached by love and kindness. John knew this and, in his living and dying, showed his faith in it. It was this which went out from him, touching all classes of people, all colors and castes and creeds. It echoed in the hearts of all, as in one heart—proof that all variety of men belong to one human family.

It came as a relief in a terrible time of the world, when some were saying that man was incapable of reason and unable to control his destiny. It said there was a chance and that we should not despair. It gave mankind a glimpse of how the world would look if it were governed by love. And it was this glimpse which had brought all ages and faiths of men into the piazza to look up at the window of the man whose life and death, bearing witness of this truth, was a miracle of our age . . .

"Professor, we're ready."

"*Ah sì?*"

Manzù turned to once again force himself to look at the object in the bed.

"Then take it off—now."

The mask came easily and well. After that, they lifted away the cast of the hand which came less freely. These were the negatives for the wax copies which would be cast into bronze. Carefully, Mauro wrapped them in cotton batting and placed them in the basket. It was finished, at last, and as they left the room Manzù felt a terrible thirst. So he spoke to Guido Gusso, the Pope's valet and chauffeur.

"Listen," he said. "I know that you can't drink here because there's nothing. But if somewhere nearby there's a drop of cognac —"

"Why?"

"Eh, I'd gladly drink it."

"Why do you say 'There's nothing here?'"

"Eh, no, because once when I felt ill, Capovilla said 'Give him a cognac.' But Giovanni said: 'No, no — bring him a nice tea.' So I drank a tea you brought. But when you had left the room, Giovanni said to me: 'You know, Manzù, I had them bring you tea because here the cognac is not good.'"

Gusso seemed upset by this.

"No, no," he said. "You come with me, because Papa Giovanni never drank those things. Come with me and I'll give you some French cognac."

As soon as Manzù had tasted it, he said to his assistants: "Take it and drink, because this bottle was made for this moment."

All three drank together. Then they took the two baskets with the materials and mask imprints and walked out. Going down the corridor, Manzù heard a cruet crash in the chapel. In the distance, the unanswered phone was again ringing on and on, like a lost ambulance. At the apartment exit, two Swiss Guards watched them leave, their faces broken only by the slow blink of yoked oxen.

In the piazza, many people lingered on, looking up at the papal apartment with its little patch of yellow light against the night sky. Manzù looked, too, and thought of John, alone in his tiny bed in the room he would never see again. It was the hour of good-bye for everyone.

But his farewell would be said at home, in his studio, and he hurried there to begin it—a new panel for the door of St. Peter's, showing John alive and in prayer. He would do it as well as he could, cast it in bronze and then erect it before the world, to endure against age and disease and death for as long as the door and the basilica remained.

It was after midnight when he opened the studio door. There were a dozen or more panels standing upright—variations on different themes for the door. In the night light they appeared haltingly huddled together like sailboats at the start of a regatta. One of them had to go—to make room for the new panel on John—and Manzù decided it would be Death in Water, a half-finished panel showing a man drowning. So he pulled to one side, and turned it to the wall—out of the race.

He began then on a fresh clay panel, using a knife to draft the figure of John. It went easily and well—the great folds of his cape leading up to the clasped hands and the noble head bent in prayer. He wore a simple skull cap with the heavy papal tiara suspended in the top right corner. It was John, seen in the fullness of his life. To show him in the act of dying, Manzù cut the date of his death onto the panel of St. Joseph expiring from fatigue and age by the roadside. It worked well, he thought, because this old man, this saint could also have been John. He cut the date deeply—3 VI 63—and then placed flowers atop his worn staff, flowers of man's eternal virility and love.

That was all there was to do. Nothing more was needed on the door—except a prayer for all the nights and days that remained to mankind. It was in John's three words and the sculptor hastily cut them in the panel: *Pacem in Terris*.

So be it. *Addio*, dear friend.